The **AP**[*] Comparative
Government and
Politics Examination

JUST THE FACTS!

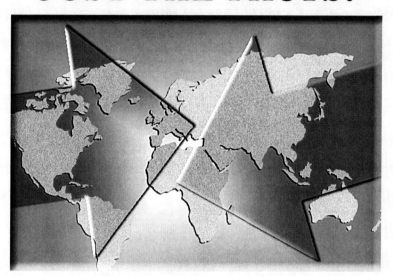

The Facts and Definitions
You Need to Know for the Exam

BY KEN WEDDING

Author of *The AP Comparative Government and
Politics Examination: What You Need to Know*

Published by College City Publications
Northfield, Minnesota

All inquiries should be addressed to:

College City Publications

925 Ivanhoe Drive

Northfield, Minnesota 55057

E-mail: *information@apcomparativegov.com*

Web site: *apcomparativegov.com*

Credits for Wikimedia Commons Images: Page 3, public domain; **Page 7**, NASA photo in the public domain; **Page 11**, Creative Commons Attribution-Share Alike 3.0 Unported, 2.5 Generic, 2.0 Generic and 1.0 Generic license; **Page 14**, Creative Commons Attribution 2.0 Generic license / public domain; **Page 18**, public domain / www.kremlin.ru, under Creative Commons Attribution 3.0 Unported Licence; **Page 23**, Creative Commons Attribution 2.0 Generic license; **Page 36**, Creative Commons Attribution/Share-Alike License; **Page 49**, Creative Commons Attribution-Share Alike 3.0 Unported license; **Page 53**, Creative Commons Attribution 2.0 Generic license; **Page 79**, Creative Commons Attribution-Share Alike 2.0 Generic license.

Images on Page 16 (left to right, top to bottom): available under OGL, CC BY-SA 2.0, CC BY 2.0, CC BY-ND 2.0, public domain, public domain, CC BY 3.0 at Wikimedia Commons and Flickr

Image on Page 47: Found at http://www.connectafricandevelopment.org/2012/05/training-opportunities-from-west-africa.html on December 18, 2013

International Standard Book No.: 978-0-9965782-0-2

PRINTED IN THE UNITED STATES OF AMERICA

JUST THE FACTS!

Thanks to Karen Waples, John Unruh-Friesen,
Susan Ikenberry, and Sarah Fisher for comments
and suggestions on an early draft.

FOREWORD

This study guide is based on the official Advanced Placement* course outline, which mostly serves as the table of contents.

This guide is organized around the official course description, using examples from appropriate countries to illustrate facts and definitions. As you work through the big ideas, remember that about one-third of the multiple choice exam questions ask about governments' structures and processes.

You should get your own copy of the official course description to accompany this guide. The course description can be downloaded at

> https://apstudent.collegeboard.org/apcourse/
> ap-comparative-government-and-politics

At that site there are links to

- a downloadable version of the official course description
- an outline of the course
- practice exam questions

For more resources, see page 122.

For more resources, see page 122.

---

* AP and Advanced Placement Program are registered trademarks of the College Entrance Examination Board, which was not involved with the production of and does not endorse this publication.

INTRODUCTION TO COMPARATIVE POLITICS (PART ONE)

BASIC VOCABULARY

Sorry about this. The political science of comparative politics comes later (see p. 78), but some jargon comes now.

> Britain's Prime Minister David Cameron had been careful ahead of [the] House of Commons vote [on attacking Syria] to make clear that the ambitions of any such intervention would be limited. Neither Britain nor the U.S. sought regime change. Regime change may yet result ... as Britons question his leadership. – Catherine Mayer, *Time* magazine, 30 August 2013

> "You either ought to change the regime or you ought to do nothing." – Donald Rumsfeld, former US Secretary of Defense, speaking to WOOD-TV in Grand Rapids, Michigan, 3 September 2013

- Do you know what a reporter is discussing when she writes about "regime change?"

- Do you know what a politician is talking about when he mentions "regime change?"

- Are those two people referring to the same thing?

- Is "regime change" for politicians and journalists what political scientists mean by "regime change?" What is a regime, anyway? (Read on.)

Political scientists do not use these terms in the same ways they are used in everyday speech. **You need to learn the language...**

THE LANGUAGE OF COMPARATIVE POLITICS

Power: the ability to direct the behavior of others through coercion, persuasion, or leadership

> There will be no end of the troubles of states, or of humanity itself, till philosophers become kings in this world, or till those we now call kings and rulers really and truly become philosophers, and political power and philosophy thus come into the same hands. – Plato

> Political power grows out the barrel of a gun. – Mao Zedong

Authority: the legal right to exercise power on behalf of the society and/or government

> Authority is not a quality one person 'has,' in the sense that he has property or physical qualities. Authority refers to an interpersonal relation in which one person looks upon another as somebody superior to him. – Erich Fromm

> All lawful authority, legislative, and executive, originates from the people. – James Burgh

4¢ Mexican stamp, issued in 1898 by the Mexican Postal Authority

Sovereignty: independent legal authority over a population in a particular place; the degree to which a state controls its own territory and independently makes and carries out policy

> Authority, without any condition and reservation, belongs to the nation. – Mustafa Kemal Atatürk

> The moon and other celestial bodies should be free for... use by all countries. No country should be permitted to advance a claim of sovereignty. – Lyndon B. Johnson

Politics: the processes through which groups of people govern themselves or are governed; activities associated with the exercise of authority

> The whole art of politics consists of directing rationally the irrationalities of men. – Reinhold Niebuhr

> Politics are too serious a matter to be left to politicians. – Charles De Gaulle

Nation: a group of people who identify themselves as belonging together because of cultural, geographic, or linguistic ties

> It is my express wish that in awarding the prizes no consideration be given to the nationality of the candidates, but that the most worthy shall receive the prize... – Alfred Nobel

> I do not call the sod under my feet my country; but language – religion – government – blood – identity in these makes men of one country. – Samuel Taylor Coleridge

State: all those people and groups within a nation-state that have power to effect change at some level of society through direct action or political participation

> The state refers to the key political institutions responsible for making, implementing, and adjudicating important policies in a country. – Mark Kesselman

> The state includes all the institutions and individuals that exercise political authority and use institutional resources to manage society's problems and affairs. – Charles Hauss

Nation-state: a territorial unit controlled by a single state and governed by a single government

> Without a country, I am not a man. – Nawaf Al-Nasir Al-Shabah

> In every particular state of the world, those nations which are strongest tend to prevail over the others; and in certain marked peculiarities the strongest tend to be the best. – Walter Bagehot

Regime: a pattern of organization for a government (often described in a constitution or supreme law)

> It is almost universally felt that when we call a country democratic we are praising it; consequently, the defenders of every kind of regime claim that it is a democracy. – George Orwell

> In South Africa, we could not have achieved our freedom and just peace without the help of people around the world... to reverse decades-long support for the Apartheid regime. – Desmond Tutu

Rule of law: a governance system that operates predictably under a known and relatively transparent set of procedural rules (laws)

> We must fight terrorism with methods that do not compromise our respect for the rule of law and human rights. – Anna Lindh

> [The rule of law] means that government in all its actions is bound by rules fixed and announced beforehand – rules which make it possible to foresee with fair certainty how the authority will use its coercive powers in given circumstances... – Friedrich A. Hayek

Government: the part of the state with legitimate public authority; the group of people and organizations that hold political authority in a state at any one time

> Government can be defined as the leadership or elite in charge of running the state. – Patrick H. O'Neil

> Government: the group of people in office at a particular time; administration. – The Oxford English Dictionary

Head of state: the chief public representative of a state

> The executive role that symbolizes and represents the people both nationally and internationally. – Patrick H. O'Neil

Head of government: the office and the person occupying the office charged with leading the operation of a government

> The country's chief political officer responsible for presenting and conducting its principal policies. – Michael J. Sodaro

Civil society: all organizations which provide avenues of public participation in society

> Business, labor and civil society organizations have skills and resources that are vital in helping to build a more robust global community. – Kofi Annan

> Nor was civil society founded merely to preserve the lives of its members; but that they might live well: for otherwise a state might be composed of slaves, or the animal creation... – Aristotle

State capacity: the ability of the government to implement its policies

> The challenge is to... create a state that has both the capacity and willingness to mobilize resources, exercise political power, control its territory, manage the economy, implement policy, and promote human welfare... – The World Bank

> The ability of the state to wield power to carry out basic tasks, such as defending territory, making and enforcing rules, collecting taxes, and managing the economy. – Patrick H. O'Neil

The head of state in the UK is...? In 2015, it was Queen Elizabeth II.

Legitimacy: the belief that a regime is a proper one and that the government has a right to exercise authority

Some possible ways to earn legitimacy:

- representative government
- rule of law
- history of stable and successful government
- widely shared sense of national identity
- protection of individual liberty
- provision of adequate standard of living
- success in state-sponsored economic growth
- honest and transparent political system
- successful political integration
- adequate social welfare system available to all
- government responsiveness to public opinion
- protection from forces outside the nation-state
- achievements in war, technology, science, athletics, fine arts, or other valued behavior
- heroic/charismatic leadership

Compliance—not legitimacy—can be achieved through surveillance, threats, and the use of force.

And then there's this point (taken directly from the official course description):

Students should learn about "the general political and economic permeability of national borders…"

Permeability: The ability of a substance to allow another substance to pass through it… – The Free Online Dictionary

Permeable borders? Nation-states go to great lengths to secure their borders. How can they be permeable?

Well, think about some of the things that get through borders.

refugees	jobs
pollution	Facebook
Komatsu Ltd	World of Warfare
petroleum	Médecins Sans Frontières
heroin	Human Rights Watch
invasive species	tourists
H1N1 virus	typhoons
Kalashnikovs	Olympics
fundamentalism	water
wars	organized crime
Miley Cyrus	IMF
Al Jazeera	euros
NGOs	investments
technology	Confucius Institutes
and …	political ideas (e.g., democratization)

A MEGA-CONCEPT

If nations are primary actors on the world stage, they must be independent and autonomous. In other words, sovereign.

Sovereign: the effective ruler of a geographic territory
Historically the sovereign was a monarch; today it is a characteristic of most governments

Sovereign state: The Treaties of Westphalia in 1648 recognized some nation-states and their sovereign rulers as legitimate and independent actors in European politics. Empires like the Roman one or the Holy Roman one were no longer the top dogs in European politics.

Sovereignty: independent legal authority over a population in a particular place; the degree to which a state controls its own territory and independently makes and carries out policy

(This should sound familiar.)

In the real world of international relations, **sovereignty** is a variable, not a discrete characteristic of nation-states. Some nation-states have greater **capacity** than others and therefore greater sovereignty. Some nation-states are parts of supranational organizations that assume some of member nation-states' sovereignty. (See definitions above and on the next page.)

Capacity: the degree to which a state or government is able to implement its policies (i.e., able to exercise **sovereignty**)

(This should sound familiar, too.)

Economically and politically **permeable** borders limit **sovereignty**. Anything that crosses a nation-state's borders without official sanction demonstrates a limit to that nation-state's **capacity** and **sovereignty**.

Supranational (with powers greater than the nation-state), **transnational** (operating beyond a nation-state's borders), and **international organizations** (nation-states are members) limit **sovereignty** of nation-states.

Multi-national corporations exercise economic and political powers that challenge the **sovereignty** and limit the **capacity** of nation-states.

International organization:	United Nations
Transnational organization:	NATO or LUKOIL
Supranational organization:	European Union

Does any nation-state have total sovereignty?

No. Even states with the greatest capacity on earth are limited in what they can do.

LUKOIL is "a major international vertically-integrated oil and gas company" that is responsible for 16.3% of Russian oil production and 16.7% of Russian oil refining — and is the owner of this service station in New York.

NOW, GO SPEAK SOME
COMPARATIVE POLITICAL SCIENCE!

A. Can a legitimate regime be sovereign?

B. Can a nation be a nation-state?

C. Can a government have power without authority?

D. Does effective rule of law make legitimacy harder to achieve?

E. Is there a link between state capacity and sovereignty?

F. Can a sovereign nation-state have permeable borders?

G. Does a free civil society limit the legitimacy of a regime?

ANSWERS:

A. Yes and legitimacy aids sovereignty.

B. If the borders of the group coincide with the borders of the nation state.

C. Powerful forces (the military) can impose government on a nation state without authority or legitimacy.

D. No. In fact it makes legitimacy easier to earn.

E. If a nation state is unable for economic or technical reasons to do what it desires, sovereignty is reduced.

F. Yes. Nearly all do.

G. In fact, like effective rule of law, free civil society strengthens legitimacy.

SOVEREIGNTY, AUTHORITY, AND POWER

The second section of the course outline focuses on mega-concepts.

Political culture: the collection of history, values, beliefs, assumptions, attitudes, traditions, and symbols that define and influence political behavior within a nation-state

- The revolutionary **history** of independent Mexico means that people expect governments to remain true to the principles of equality, secularism, and government direction of the economy.

- The **values** developed over centuries of limited government in the United Kingdom ensure the existence of fair trials without a constitution.

- The **beliefs** of Shia Islam trump modern desires for unrestricted representative government in Iran.

- Most Russians **assume** that it's their duty to serve the nation.

- Many Nigerians have an **attitude** that government and politics are corrupt and that anyone related to those in power deserves a fair share of "profits."

- **Traditionally**, political power in Russia has been exercised from the top, not from the grassroots up.

- In China, the color red has become a **symbol** for independence and progress, as well as for the Communist Party.

Political cultures often include ideologies.

Ideology: a set of basic beliefs about political, economic, social and cultural affairs that its advocates believe is comprehensive and coherent; **ideologies** vary in comprehensiveness and coherence

Because **ideologies** are not always comprehensive and coherent, people with political authority who follow ideologies, often try to modify reality to fit their set of basic beliefs or resort to **pragmatism**.

Pragmatism: the practice of taking action or making policy dictated by consideration of the immediate practical consequences rather than by theory or dogma (ideology)

Compare Mao Zedong's policies during the Great Leap Forward with Deng Xiaoping's policies during the Four Modernizations. Who was pragmatic?

ANSWER: Mao Zedong's government tried, during the Great Leap Forward, to put into practice many things that were consistent with Communist ideology. Deng Xiaoping, after Mao's death, seemed willing to implement reforms that worked to create economic growth, even if they weren't strictly Communist. As a pragmatist, Deng was quoted as saying, "What does it matter if a cat is white or black, as long as it catches mice."

Ideologies or near-ideologies often involve describing preferred relationships between governments and economies.

Marxism: an analysis of social and economic relationships that assumes the preeminence of exploitation by some social classes and the need for government intervention to alleviate the exploitation.

Socialism: a political/economic system in which the government plays a major role (usually ownership) in determining the use of productive resources and the allocation of valuable goods and services; may be democratic or authoritarian

Liberalism: a set of beliefs that favors a limited role of government in the economy and people's lives; emphasizes individual freedoms

Capitalism: an economic system that emphasizes private property rights and market mechanisms

Free market economics: a belief that economic decisions should be made by the uninhibited functioning of markets

Supply side economics: a set of beliefs that asserts that freeing producers and suppliers of economic goods from taxation and regulation can resolve economic problems and promote economic growth

Political scientists identify the process through which people become part of their political culture as **political socialization**. This is another important part of political culture. How do people learn to function in a political system? How do they learn the rules of proper behavior?

Families are the earliest agents of **political socialization**. Schools, respected adults, peers, socially sanctioned groups and activities, employers, interactions with social and government agents, and media are some of the other agents of **political socialization**.

Five of the seven members of the Standing Committee of China's Communist Party are sons of revolutionary heroes or military commanders.

POLITICAL INSTITUTIONS

Most political systems create and describe their regimes in constitutions. In the 21st century, nearly every regime invokes a **constitution** as evidence of legitimacy and rule of law.

Constitution: a supreme law that defines the structure of a nation-state's regime and the legal processes governments must follow

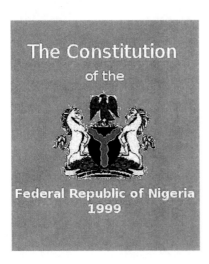

GOVERNMENTAL STRUCTURE

The structure of a regime defined in a constitution is the general outline of the **executive, legislative,** and **judicial** institutions and their powers (to use John Locke's tripartite organization).

Executive institutions: the people and agencies, which implement or execute public policy; people or groups in charge of the executive are the government

- **UK:** Prime Minister, elected by the legislature, is the chief executive or head of government; cabinet members picked by the PM are heads of government ministries that carry out policy decisions made by Parliamentary majority.

- **Russia:** Executive powers are shared by popularly elected president and presidentially appointed premier; presidential and premier's cabinet members are heads of government ministries; policies are made by legislature and president.

- **China:** Premier, named by president and national legislature, is head of government; cabinet ministers direct ministries to implement policy; president, head of state, is also head of the Communist Party of China (CPC) and its Politburo Standing Committee, where all significant policy decisions are made.

- **Nigeria:** President is head of state and head of government; presidentially appointed (and legislatively approved) cabinet members head ministries to implement and administer policies made by the legislature and the president.

- **Mexico:** President is head of state and head of government; cabinet members appointed by the president lead ministries that carry out policy decisions made by the president and the legislature.

🏳 **Iran**: Popularly elected president is head of government; president's cabinet appointees are approved by the legislature and the Supreme Leader to carry out policies which are approved by the legislature and the Supreme Leader.

Legislative institutions: the public body (or bodies) with the authority to make, amend, and repeal statutory laws as well as impose taxes and authorize public spending for a political unit

Parliamentary government: a system of governance in which the head of government is chosen by and serves at the pleasure of the legislature

Congressional government: a system of governance in which the head of government is separate from the legislature

🏳 **UK**: Bicameral legislature—lower House of Commons elected from single member districts by pluralities holds all significant legislative power and authority; upper House of Lords appointed by monarch as directed by the government (a few hereditary seats remain in Lords)

🏳 **Russia**: Bicameral legislature—lower house, Duma, elected proportionally from party lists (a party must receive at least 7% of the popular vote to win any seats); upper house, the Federal Council, is appointed to represent local government units; has little more than delaying powers; dominance of Putin's United Russia party has made the legislature a voice of the president

- **China**: Unicameral legislature—the National People's Congress has nearly 3,000 members; legislators are chosen by provincial legislatures with the approval of Communist Party officials; the NPC approves (with rare "no" votes) decrees and policies made by its Central Committee and that Central Committee's Standing Committee in the year since the NPC's last meeting

- **Nigeria**: Bicameral legislature—the House of Representatives includes 360 members elected in plurality elections from single member districts; 109 Senators are elected in plurality elections from single member districts (three Senators from each state and one from the Federal Capital Territory of Abuja); corruption and divisive self-interests have made it difficult for the legislature to wield any of its authority in shaping national policy

- **Mexico**: Bicameral legislature—300 members of the Chamber of Deputies are elected from single member districts by pluralities and 200 others are elected proportionally by party lists; 96 Senators are elected directly in state and federal territory elections and 32 are chosen from lists of the party that won the second most votes in each state (this ensures that the parties will win seats even in states where they're not the most popular); PRI dominance and the failure of PAN to win majorities have made the legislature secondary to the president in policy making

- **Iran**: Unicameral legislature—the Majlis has 290 members elected by majorities in (if necessary) two-round elections in single member districts; all of its actions must be approved by the Supreme Leader and the Guardian Council; on rare occasions it comes into conflict with the president, but has little power or authority compared to the executive

Judicial institutions: the collection of courts in a regime with the authority to interpret laws (statute and common)

- **UK:** The legal system is a combination of common law and civil law systems. Decisions can be appealed to higher courts, but *stare decisis* is a powerful tradition; only the Supreme Court can negate laws passed by Parliament and then only laws that are deemed to contradict the EU human rights declaration.

- **Russia:** The judiciary is made up of a Supreme Court and lower courts; a Constitutional Court considers issues that involve possible contradictions with the constitution and can in limited circumstances negate statutes. The legal system is inquisitorial (on the Napoleonic model) and civil (based on statutes).

- **China:** The Supreme People's Court oversees the top level of appellate courts that are organized by function; lower court decisions can be appealed to higher courts. The system is a civil law system and inquisitorial.

- **Nigeria:** There are hierarchies of secular and Sharia law courts through which decisions can be appealed. While there is some role for *stare decisis* in secular courts that system is primarily an adversarial, civil law system and the Sharia system is exclusively an inquisitorial, civil law system.

- **Mexico:** The civil law system consists of a hierarchy of courts through which lower court decisions can be appealed. The Supreme Court can nullify statutes, but rarely does.

- **Iran:** the system is strictly a civil law system; all judges are clergy and all deal with Sharia and civil law. Decisions can be appealed to the Supreme Court.

Rule of law: constitutionalism; a governance system operating predictably under a known and transparent set of procedural rules (laws)

- **UK:** Precedents replace a written constitution. The British system is usually cited as a prime example of a rule of law regime.

- **Russia:** The dominance of Putin and the United Russia party has overwhelmed the system. Decisions made behind the scenes become public only when implemented; political opponents of those in power are regularly harassed and jailed; the secretive nature of the president's power ministry cabinet adds to a lack of transparency. While commercial law is more transparent, government ownership of major corporations and media means that rule of law is tenuous.

The scales of justice, located in London atop the Central Criminal Court of England and Wales, commonly known as the Old Bailey from the street on which it stands

- **China:** Rule of law is mostly replaced by rule of the Communist Party. Courts hold secret and non-public sessions; decisions are easy for outside observers to predict. Even in commercial law, foreign investors risk having the wrong partners in the nearly invisible *guanxi* patron-client system or violating rules that apply only to them.

- **Nigeria:** Large scale political disputes about the details of legislation and party politics demonstrate respect for rule of law, but the dominance of the president and his administration as well as secret back room deals within political parties subvert it. Courts appear open, but delays and corruption within the police and courts undermine their legitimacy.

- **Mexico:** Inquisitorial courts are often opaque rather than transparent; corruption within law enforcement means that delays in prosecution reduce the effectiveness of rule of law. Politically, the patron-client networks make it difficult to see where decisions are made and who benefits even when laws and policies are legislated.

- **Iran:** The constitution calls for rule of Sharia law through the interpretation of religious legal scholars, whose interpretations are not all the same. Judges' decisions involving political matters are unpredictable. Dissenters and opponents of those with power are subject to persecution and imprisonment.

Judicial review: In **common law systems**, courts have the authority to modify or nullify the actions of legislatures, executives, and lower courts; these decisions create precedents that are preserved through stare decisis.

> **Stare decisis:** the legal principle that judges should respect and follow precedents whenever possible

In **civil or statutory law systems**, laws are enacted by legislative or regulatory bodies and higher courts can reverse or modify lower court decisions without creating precedents for future cases.

- **UK:** Common law system gives courts power except over Parliament, whose decisions are final except in human rights cases under EU law.

- **Russia:** Court decisions can be appealed, but only the Constitutional Court can overrule the legislature or executive policies, and it doesn't.

- **China:** While higher courts can modify or negate lower court rulings, the laws and policies approved by the National People's Congress are not reviewable.

- **Nigeria:** A Constitutional Court can review and negate legislation and executive policies and other high courts can review lower court decisions.

- **Mexico:** The Supreme Court can nullify legislation and executive policies, but rarely does. Decisions can be appealed from lower courts.

- **Iran:** The Supreme Leader can nullify legislation and policy, not the courts.

Civil law systems: Russia, China, Mexico, and Iran

Combined common law and civil law systems: The United Kingdom and Nigeria

Constitutions or basic laws create things other than structures of a regime. They also

* define citizenship
* outline the limits of governmental authority
* identify the obligations of government to the citizens
* describe the rights and obligations of citizens

CITIZENSHIP

Citizen: a member of a nation-state who is legally entitled to full civil rights and is legally obliged to perform defined public duties

GOVERNMENT LIMITS

Civil rights and civil liberties: freedoms protected by the state from unwarranted infringement by governments and private organizations

They ensure (in liberal states) citizens' ability to participate in the civil and political life of the society and the state.

ELECTORAL PROCESSES

The third thing created by constitutions are **electoral systems,** the institutions and procedures within which votes are cast and counted in a representative regime.

Universal suffrage: the right to vote of every adult citizen except those who are individually excluded from voting (dependents and incarcerated criminals, for example)

Limited suffrage: a system in which only a subset of citizens is granted the right to vote

Plurality election: an electoral system that declares a candidate receiving the most votes as the winner (also called a "first past the post" system)

Majority election: an electoral system that requires winners to receive the majority of votes cast (sometimes a majority of eligible voters)

This often requires secondary voting between the top candidates who did not receive a majority

Proportional election: an electoral system in which a party's candidates win office in proportion to the percentages of votes won by the party (there is usually a minimum percentage a party is required to receive before any of its candidates are elected)

Ranked choice voting: voters rank all candidates by their preferences

If a voter's first choice candidate is not elected, his or her second choice candidate gets the vote, etc.

SEPARATION/FUSION OF POWERS

Locke and Montesquieu wrote that every political system must legislate, administer, and adjudicate.

Many (but not all) liberal, representative regimes create separate institutions for each function.

Separation of powers: a system of governance in which political power and duties are divided into several subdivisions (or branches) so that each has different responsibilities

Fusion of powers: a system of governance in which the authority of government is concentrated in one body

Checks and balances: a system of governance in which each of the major subdivisions (or branches) can restrain the political power of at least one of the others

What about *illiberal* states?

Illiberal states are those that have the trappings of a constitution, elections, and rule of law but in fact have only a symbolic constitution, non-competitive elections, and a façade that appears to be rule of law. The government regularly ignores human rights and treats citizens as subjects.

Power distribution in relevant case studies:

- **UK:** Classic example of **fusion** of power— executive is chosen by and is part of the legislature; courts are now separate from the legislature, but the new Supreme Court, which can nullify Parliamentary laws, handles only human rights cases under EU treaties.

- **Russia:** Clear constitutional **separation** of powers—BUT dominance of Putin and United Russia in executive and legislative branches and presidential appointment of the highest court negate the checks and balances.

- **China:** The constitutional **separation** of powers AND **fusion** of the Communist Party with the government hands all power to the party.

- **Nigeria:** Constitutional **separation** of powers—BUT oil income (80%+ of government revenue) flows through president's office and focuses power in the executive.

- **Mexico:** Constitutional **separation** of powers—divided government during the last three sexenios demonstrates real system of checks and balances; judiciary weak.

- **Iran:** Constitutional **separation** of duties—BUT guarantee of "veto" power to Supreme Leader and politically active clerics negate any sense of checks and balances beyond clerical power.

Legislatures / Legislators

Legislatures in relevant case studies:

- **UK:** Bicameral—House of Lords and House of Commons; the quintessential **parliamentary** system; head of government (the Prime Minister) is chosen by the House of Commons majority; House of Lords holds only minor power

- **Russia:** Bicameral—Federation Council and State Duma; a presidential/ congressional system; head of government, not necessarily from legislature, is appointed by president (head of state); Federation Council holds only minor power

- **China:** Unicameral—National People's Congress (NPC); presidential system; head of government elected by the NPC (Communist Party nominee)

- **Nigeria:** Bicameral—Senate and House of Representatives; presidential/congressional system; popularly elected president is head of government

- **Mexico:** Bicameral—Senate and Chamber of Deputies; presidential/congressional system; popularly elected president is head of government

- **Iran:** Unicameral—Islamic Consultative Assembly of Iran (aka *Majlis*); neo-presidential system; nationally elected president is head of government and subject to the authority of the head of state (the Supreme Leader)

Administrators

Executive: the people and agencies which implement or execute government policy

- In a **parliamentary system**, the head of government is chosen by a majority in the legislature and holds executive and legislative power
- In a **presidential system**, the head of government is chosen independently of the legislature and holds executive, but not legislative power

Technically, the two top executive positions in a nation-state are the **head of state** and **the head of government**.

In many regimes, one person holds both positions. In the **Federal Republic of Nigeria** and the **United Mexican States (Mexico)**, the president is both head of state and head of government.

In the **UK**, the monarch is the head of state, while the prime minister is the head of government. That separation is mirrored in **Russia** where the president is head of state and the prime minister (the Chairman of the Government of the Russian Federation) is the head of government. A similar separation of positions exists in the **People's Republic of China (PRC)** where the president is head of state and the premier is head of government.

The separation of the positions is slightly different in **The Islamic Republic of Iran** where the Supreme Leader is the head of state and the president is the head of government.

The head of government is usually the executive leading a **cabinet** of ministers each charged with a specific area of responsibility (e.g., foreign affairs, military, justice, health, education, local affairs, etc.)

Cabinet: the group of ministers who direct administrative bureaucracies (ministries or departments), which is accountable to the head of government

In parliamentary systems, the head of government and the cabinet are referred to as the government.

Bureaucracy: a hierarchically structured organization charged with carrying out the policies determined by those with political authority

Bureaucrats are **civil servants** who, in theory*, have been hired for their technical expertise, specialized knowledge, and special skills and/or because they performed well on objectively fair assessments of their abilities and knowledge (civil service tests). They are often referred to as **technocrats** because of their specialized, non-political knowledge and skills.

Their jobs are to carry out or implement public policy made by people with political authority. They are supposed to be separated from making policy** by their positions in an organization where policy and directions come from the top leaders, who are political policy makers.

---

*   Many (most?) bureaucratic systems hire people because of their political connections.

** Bureaucrats, especially technical experts, often wield great influence over policies adopted by governments and legislatures.

Courts / Judges

Judiciary: the set of institutions that are created to

- interpret the application of public laws and policies
- settle public disputes in the nation-state
- enforce criminal law

If it is functioning ideally (a normative description), the judiciary plays a large role in maintaining a rule of law.

Rule of law: constitutionalism; a governance system operating predictably under a known and transparent set of procedural rules (laws)

A major responsibility of an effective (an empirical description) judiciary is to interpret **statute law** or **administrative regulations** as they are applied.

In some legal systems the judiciary must also interpret the application of **common law** and **precedent**.

Nearly all systems allow appeals to higher courts.

[For more, refer to pages 18-25 on "Constitutions."]

Besides distinguishing between statutory (civil law) systems and common law systems, it is important (a normative description) to distinguish between **inquisitorial** and **adversarial** legal systems.

Inquisitorial (non-adversarial) legal system:
a system, especially in criminal law, in which the court is responsible for investigating cases and making judgments that legally resolve them

The court is charged with determining the facts of cases and the proper application of statutory law.

Adversarial legal system: a system in which the parties to a legal case present (or more often hire attorneys to present) their interpretation of the case to an impartial court (a judge and/or jury) for determination of facts and application of laws

Inquisitorial courts are more likely in civil or statutory law systems (like those in Mexico, China, and Russia). **Adversarial courts** are more likely in common law systems like the UK or Nigeria.

Sharia legal system: Iran relies on a Sharia system.

Judges are clerics; personal oral testimony is practically the only "evidence" accepted; and decisions are unique to each case and do not create precedents. Decisions must be based on Islamic law (written and oral); most decisions can be appealed to higher courts.

Other Institutions

Military: armed forces that are used to protect the nation-state against possible or actual invasion by the military forces of other nations; also used to maintain the power of the government within the nation-state's borders; also used to project the power of the nation-state beyond its borders by displays of military might and technology

- ⚑ **UK:** Officially Her Majesty's Armed Forces encompass three professional uniformed services: The Naval Service, the British Army, and the Royal Air Force. The British military has been non-political since the 17th century.

- ⚑ **Russia:** The military consists of Russian Ground Forces, the Russian Navy, the Russian Air Force, the Strategic Missile Troops, the Russian Aerospace Defense Forces, and the Russian Airborne Troops. The military was actively involved in the turmoil at the end of the Soviet Union and the beginning of the Russian Federation, but except at the highest levels of military, government, and politics, where it lobbies, the military has not been political since.

- ⚑ **China:** The People's Liberation Army (PLA) is comprised of four main services: the PLA Ground Force, the PLA Navy, the PLA Air Force, and the Second Artillery Corps (strategic missile force). The PLA is the arm of the Communist Party. It was vital in putting down the protests and unrest of 1989. Since then it has been co-opted by civilian/party leaders through increased military budgets and expanding missile and space programs.

- ⚑ **Nigeria:** The military is made up of the Army, the Navy, and the Air Force. The military has been a political force throughout the independence period. It fought the civil war, twice overthrew elected governments and ruled the country, military officers overthrew other military rulers several times, and attempted at least three times to establish new civilian regimes. It remains a political force to be reckoned with.

🏴 **Mexico:** The armed forces consist of the Army and the Navy; air forces are included in the Army. The Mexican military has generally been non-political. In recent years the army has been called upon to combat heavily armed drug cartels.

The Supreme Leader and Commander-in-Chief of the Armed Forces meeting with commanders of the Armed Forces of the Islamic Republic of Iran

▶ **Iran:** The military is made up of the Army, the Navy, the Air Force, the Air Defense Force, the Guardians of the Islamic Revolution (aka Revolutionary Guards, which includes land, sea, air forces and *Quds* or special forces), and the *Basij*, a paramilitary force of three million combat capable people. All branches of the military, but especially the Revolutionary Guards, the *Quds*, and the *Basij*, have been active in supporting the regime.

Intelligence services: All these countries operate domestic and international intelligence programs that have, in the last decade, expanded to include cyber intelligence operations. The Russian FSB, the Chinese MSS, and the Iranian MOIS are politically the most powerful and intrusive.

CITIZENS, SOCIETY, AND STATE

The fourth part of the course outline emphasizes the relationships between people, their organizations, and the state.

POLITICAL SYSTEMS

Political party: an organized group of people with the primary purpose of electing some of its members to government office

> In some political cultures, electing members to public office is also (primarily?) a way to procure a share of state revenues and/or bribes.

Interest aggregation: ways in which demands of citizens and groups are amalgamated into proposed policy packages by interest groups

In most systems **political parties** are organizations used to aggregate common interests for political purposes.

Political parties also serve as vehicles for promoting and implementing ideologies, e.g., the Communist Party of China (at least in the past).

Interest groups are distinguished from political parties because their primary goal is to influence policy making, not to elect people to public office.

One-party political systems: Sometimes a party has enough power, authority, and/or legitimacy to have exclusive control of government and politics (e.g., the People's Republic of China).

Dominant party political systems: In some political systems there is more than one party, but one party is so dominant that it is able to virtually monopolize political power (e.g., Mexico before 2000 and Russia after 2000).

Two-party political systems: In a few political systems, two competitive parties are popular and powerful enough to leave smaller parties without political power most of the time (e.g., the UK before 2010).

Multiple party political systems: In most political systems that have competitive elections, there are more than two parties that have a realistic chance of earning a share of political power.

> **Ambiguity**: Most nation-states do **not** fit neatly into these categories. In **China**, the Communist Party recognizes eight other political parties. The coalition government in the **UK** and the rising power of the SNP (see p. 57) demonstrate the importance of more than two parties. Regional parties in **Nigeria** have geographically limited success, but little power at a national level. **Iran** discourages the formation of political parties since "everyone" is loyal to Islam, the Supreme Leader, and the nation-state.

Interest groups: organizations created to influence policy makers

Interest groups provide information and arguments to support the policy outcomes they prefer. This activity takes place in a variety of settings in a political culture. They also offer money and benefits to decision-makers (not always legally).

- ⚑ **UK:** Interest groups concentrate their lobbying efforts on the top levels of the government and ministries; lesser efforts are made to influence public opinion.

- ⚑ **Russia:** Interest groups need personal relationships with people or patrons within the power elite of United Russia or the *siloviki* (power ministries).

- ⚑ **China**: Power flows from the top down so "lobbying" has to be done at the highest appropriate levels of the party.

- ⚑ **Nigeria:** Power is concentrated in the national government and lobbying must be done in a collection of patron-client systems divided by ethnic and geographic divisions.

- ⚑ **Mexico:** Multiple patron-client networks, strong parties, executive and legislative power centers and the non-reelection principle mean that lobbying must be done in many places, at many levels in the political system.

- ⚑ **Iran:** Clerical elites in government and the economy are the only targets of lobbying, which is largely done out of the public arena.

Political recruitment: the processes by which people are encouraged and chosen to become members of a political elite within a political system or state

- **UK:** The political and bureaucratic elites come from well-educated and wealthy backgrounds. Political elites are veteran party or union activists and candidates.

- **Russia:** Political elites have close associations with the internal security services or the administration of state-owned enterprises. Technical educations are the ones most represented; bureaucratic elites are well educated and highly skilled; all have links to patrons.

- **China**: Communist Party membership is carefully chosen with an eye to approved civic behavior and loyalty. Patron-client and family connections are vital; top bureaucrats have both great skills and great connections (*guanxi*).

- **Nigeria:** Political elites are well educated and connected within their ethnic groups; experience in party politics and local government is common; connections to military elite are helpful.

- **Mexico:** Political and bureaucratic elites are well educated in technical fields; being a loyal client to a powerful patron is vital.

- **Iran:** Nearly all the political elite are clerics; networking among the top clerics is important. The bureaucratic elite are highly educated in technical fields. Military leaders, like soldiers everywhere, form powerful links with one another. Patrons are important to all.

ELECTORAL SYSTEMS

Plurality elections: also called "first past the post" systems because the candidate with the most votes (not necessarily a majority) is elected from a single-member district; voters choose one candidate from those offered; does not necessarily represent minority interests

> **Single-member districts**: voting constituencies from which only one candidate is selected in each election

> **Multi-member districts**: voting constituencies from which more than one candidate is selected in each election

Majority elections: also called "second ballot" systems because if no candidate wins a majority in the original balloting, a second round of voting is required in which voters choose from among the more successful candidates from the first round; voters choose one candidate from those offered in each round; rely on single-member districts

Proportional elections: elections in which groups of voters are represented in the elected body in proportion to the numbers of votes in a multi-member constituency.

- **Party list systems**: Voters indicate party preference; parties select ranked lists of candidates.

- **Ranked choice systems**: Also called single transferable vote, in this system voters indicate their 1st, 2nd, 3rd, etc., choices. If a voter's 1st choice candidate is unsuccessful that vote is awarded to the voter's 2nd choice candidate, etc.

- **UK:** Plurality system in single-member districts
- **Russia:** President elected by majority in two-round system; lower house of the legislature elected by party list proportional system; upper house appointed by local governments
- **China:** President and legislature chosen by indirect methods at the direction of the Communist Party
- **Nigeria:** President elected by majority in a two-round election, if necessary; legislators (representatives and senators) chosen by pluralities in single-member districts
- **Mexico:** President elected by plurality; 60% of Chamber of Deputies elected by pluralities in single-member districts; 40% of deputies elected proportionally from 40-member constituencies. Exceptions prevent any party from winning more than 60% of the Chamber of Deputies seats. A total of 25% of Chamber of Senators are elected nationwide by proportional, party list system; 75% of senators are elected from three-candidate constituencies representing states (two seats go to the party earning a plurality in the state; one seat goes to the party earning the 2nd highest vote total).
- **Iran:** Two-round majority required for president and legislators (single-member districts); candidates must be approved by Guardian Council

DIVISIONS WITHIN NATION-STATES

Cleavage: a factor that separates groups within a society; may be cultural, historic, geographic, economic, ethnic, racial, etc.

The wider, deeper, and more numerous the cleavages, the less unified the society. Cleavages which coincide with one another can reinforce each other. Cleavages that don't coincide but cut across each other can weaken the divisions between groups.

- ⚑ **UK:** The major cleavage in the UK is the social class cleavage, however the rule of law, widely held value of justice, the tradition of *noblesse oblige*, and the social welfare system make the cleavage less politically relevant than it might be. Geographic cleavages, coinciding with archaic national (ethnic) cleavages create politically relevant divisions between England, Scotland, Wales, and Northern Ireland. Religion separates Protestants from Catholics in Northern Ireland and that becomes a politically important cleavage.

- ⚑ **Russia:** National and religious factors create politically relevant cleavages especially in the southern regions of the nation-state. Since political power is concentrated in Moscow and St. Petersburg, there's an important cleavage between those western urban areas and the rest of the country. Wealth and social class differences are lesser cleavages.

- **China:** The most politically important cleavage in China is the one that divides urban from rural residents. Geography and national (ethnic) differences reinforce the cleavages that define political conflicts in Tibet and Xinjiang. More and more the cleavage between wealthy and well-educated Chinese and others is becoming politically important.

- **Nigeria:** National (ethnic), geographic, religious, and cultural cleavages coincide across the country, strengthening the divisions among people and making political unity less and less likely. The urban-rural cleavage is important and cuts across many of the other divisions, but its power cannot moderate the others. Social class cleavages are also politically relevant.

- **Mexico:** Ethnic divisions are politically important as are the cleavages that separate people in Mexico City from those in the rest of the country. Social class and education create divisions that are politically important, but most cleavages are moderated by patron-client networks.

- **Iran:** The dominance of Shia Islam creates a unity that overwhelms nearly all national (ethnic) differences. There is a cleavage that divides the religiously educated clerics from the technically educated university and trade school graduates, but the regime gives nearly all power to the clerics. Social class divisions create groups with very different political values.

Civil society: all those organizations outside of government and (according to some authorities) commercial arenas, which provide avenues of public participation in society; participation need **not** be blatantly political

Civil society includes everything from religious congregations to football clubs to spontaneous protests to mutual aid societies for recent urban "immigrants" to political parties to motorcycle clubs.

- ▶ **UK:** Civil society is open and nearly unfettered by the government, except in cases of suspected terrorism. Groups are free to lobby the government and parties. Unions are an important part of the Labour Party.

- ▶ **Russia:** Civil society is freer than under Soviet Union, but since 2012 (Putin's new presidency) groups with connections to international organizations have been prosecuted and persecuted. Lobbying is a risky business if it is in opposition to government policy.

- ▶ **China:** Virtually no independent civil society exists. Communist Party and government go to great lengths to be in control of all civic organizations. Businesses are often exceptions, but even foreign businesses have to allow official unions and party cadres to keep tabs on workers and bosses.

- ▶ **Nigeria:** Widespread civil society activity exists, especially ethnic groups and religious organizations. Some professional associations have some influence primarily because their leaders are close to powerful politicians. Few civil society groups bridge ethnic cleavages.

- ▶ **Mexico:** There is a growing civil society, especially within growing middle classes. However, they have little influence because of the power of political parties.

▶ **Iran:** Civil society groups, if they are **not** suspected of being political, are tolerated. Political parties are discouraged. Most of the society is organized around mosques and local imams

> International civil society (NGOs): examples are Amnesty International, Human Rights Watch, the International Committee of the Red Cross, the Carter Center, CARE International, Oxfam International, World Vision International, Doctors Without Borders, and Greenpeace. Groups seek to pursue their goals in cooperation with organizations within nation-states. Their relations with governments are determined by whether or not the international groups' goals are aligned with government goals.

POLITICAL ACTION

Political participation: the actions by citizens that involve them in the process of selecting leaders, making policies, or influencing public actions

In most political systems, few people do anything more to participate in government than to vote.

Political parties are likely vehicles for participation. Advocacy for political preferences is a common incentive. The material rewards for participation, because of corruption, are powerful incentives for participation. Self-protection or the protection of a group also motivates political participation. Coerced participation is not intended to influence policy but to support the government or regime.

- ⚑ **UK:** Voter turnout in general elections averages over 70%. A small number of activists are involved in the three largest parties. Individuals and civil society groups advocate positions with the public and the government. There is a long history of protest movements.

- ⚑ **Russia:** Voter turnout in presidential elections averages 68%, in legislative elections 60%. Political parties have been encouraged and tolerated since 1990; United Russia and its civil society adjuncts have been most successful. There is little or no tradition of individual civic activity or advocacy; advocacy actions opposed to government positions are suppressed.

- ⚑ **China:** There are a few competitive elections at the rural village level. Democratic centralism means that policy decisions are made at the top of the regime and are to be accepted by citizens. Independent political activity is suppressed, individuals jailed. Communist Party membership is available to a few approved people.

- **Nigeria:** Voter turnout in presidential elections since 1999 averages 58%, in legislative elections, 54%. There are a small number of activists in many parties and large numbers of office holders and public employees. Ethnic societies support and protect members. Terrorism is a factor in the north and Niger Delta.

- **Mexico:** Voter turnout in presidential elections since 1988 averages 63%, in legislative elections 54%. Parties organize turnouts of large numbers of people for elections and for public demonstrations.

- **Iran:** Voter turnout in the last two presidential elections averaged nearly 80%, for the last two legislative elections 60%. Other independent participation is discouraged; government-organized demonstrations are allowed.

Voter casts his ballot in the 2013 presidential election in Iran

Social movements: loosely organized, populist phenomena

There are few membership lists to indicate how many people support a movement. Political actions range from well-organized lobbying to nearly spontaneous demonstrations; social media is often important for organizing. Social movements often influence political parties' policy positions.

> Studying social movements is difficult for political scientists who want facts like: How many people protested the 2009 election results in Tehran? How powerful is the resistance to the World Bank's structural adjustment programs? To what extent do people want their leaders to stop climate change? Which definition of human rights do activists want implemented? How many people support the Tibetan independence movement?

▶ **UK:** There were many social movements in 20th century Britain; women's suffrage and nuclear disarmament were two of the largest. Environmental issues have motivated social movements in recent years. People are free and likely to get politically involved.

▶ **Russia:** Since the Soviet revolution, Russians have been discouraged from getting involved in social movements not controlled by civil authorities. Since the end of the Soviet Union, small scale movements, especially in environmental and human rights arenas, often with help from international NGOs, have appeared, with government opposition. Government has been breaking the links between domestic groups and international NGOs (see p. 47).

- **China:** The Communist Party and the government maintain that the only legitimate political activity is that which takes place within the party. *Falun Gong*, a religious and social movement, has been harshly suppressed. Activists campaigning for environmental, honesty in government, or human rights causes are routinely kept under surveillance and often arrested.

- **Nigeria:** There is little tradition of social movements. Military governments, ruling for half of the time since independence, did not tolerate independent social or political activities. Ethnic cleavages are often insurmountable barriers to social movements.

- **Mexico:** The revolutionary tradition was co-opted by the PRI, discouraging non-party social movements. There have been limited social movements among university students and in Mexico City concerned with human rights, transparent elections, and environmental issues.

- **Iran:** The Islamic Republic has violently suppressed anything that appeared to be a social movement. Individual activists are arrested and harassed.

Media: instrumentalities for communicating political information like books, newspapers, magazines, radio, film, television, and social media devices like blogs, YouTube, Facebook and Twitter, especially when used with cell phones

Politically important media differ widely from one political culture to another. Wealth, technology, censorship, language, and infrastructure are among the causes of the differences.

- **UK:** Books, newspapers, magazines, and broadcast media have long been the primary political media. There is intense competition in print media; broadcasting is dominated by the BBC, which has had a reputation for political neutrality until recently. Text messaging and Twitter have become vital for spreading ideas and event planning. There has been little government interference, even with the Official Secrets Act.

- **Russia:** Books, newspapers, film, radio and television have been vital political media in the 21st century. All were firmly under state control during Soviet times. Some independent media emerged after 1990, but the central government has regained much of the lost control. Cell phones, text messaging, and Twitter-like tools have been important for dissidents and are under partial government control.

- **China:** The Communist Party has spent much time, energy, and technology to maintain control of all media and use it for the benefit of the regime. There are no independent print or broadcast media and tight controls on the Internet, with thousands employed to monitor and manage its use. A Twitter-like system has been used by dissidents for organizing some demonstrations.

- **Nigeria:** Language diversity has limited the effect of English-language press and television (except for educated, urban elite). Radio broadcasts in local languages or pidgin are very effective vehicles for political information. Cell phones are politically potent: the text messaging campaign against 2002's Miss World competition may have been world's first successful political protest organized with cell phones.

- **Mexico:** Political media are tolerated, although governments have interfered at times. There is an oligopolistic competition in broadcast media; print media is relatively unimportant. Cell phones and Twitter-like mechanisms are becoming more important for organizing.

- **Iran:** The Islamic Republic expends great resources to control media, which often self-censor to avoid government interference. Government-run broadcast media are dominant. Great efforts have been made to prevent Internet and cell phone networks from being truly global or free of censorship.

Nigerians examine newspapers on sale at a street market

POLITICAL AND ECONOMIC CHANGE

When things change—policies, governments, or regimes—it's easier to see how a political system works.

Political change: most often a reaction to other changes; causes include economic changes, demographic changes, political competition; social change; technological change

- **Economic change:** Booms, busts, recessions, growth, structural adjustment programs like austerity, privatizations, nationalizations can bring change even to authoritarian regimes.

- **Demographic change:** Urbanization, population growth, aging of a population, changes in populations of national groups (size, education, wealth, access to public services), or even general increasing educational level can create conditions that require political change.

- **Political competition:** changes in voter preferences (realignments), new, notably effective, or charismatic leadership, results of behind-the-scenes power struggles, exposed corruption, or connections with global partners can motivate changes in governments or regimes.

- **Social change:** Widespread changes in political values or public opinion, rising level of education or sophistication, increasing mobility, or changes in basic social institutions can bring about political change.

- **Technological change:** New technologies offer new opportunities for interaction and organizing. They also demand new public policy and infrastructure. These novelties can bring about political change.

TYPES OF CHANGE

Revolution: widespread and often rapid change of regime, government, leadership, politics, institutions, social relations, and economics

> The Iranian revolution in 1979 followed the classic historical model of revolution. English, Russian, Chinese, and Mexican revolutions are far enough removed from the present to have minimal impact on today's government and politics.

Civil war: an armed uprising against a government or a regime with the goal of replacing the existing political system

> The Nigerian civil war was long ago, but the cleavages illuminated by that war are still significant.

Coup d'etat: a rapid overthrow of a governing elite by another organized elite (often a military elite)

> Nigeria has experienced several coups; Russia has recent experience with an attempted coup.

Reform: a usually gradual process of change to improve a regime or a society in ways generally agreeable to most citizens or most people with political power

All countries have experienced reform or harmful change (depending on one's perspective).

Democratization: the spread, since the 1960s, of civil liberties, the rule of law, competitive elections, and independent civil society to more and more nation-states

> Observers, some scholarly, have attributed democratization to such factors as growing wealth, a general rise in education levels, the spread of market economies, growing social equality and middle classes, more independent civil society groups, and growing global awareness of democratic values.

Illiberal democratization: An illiberal democracy is a regime in which elections are held, but citizens are not a decisive factor in governing or policy making. Restrictions on civil society and civil liberties exist, and there's a lack of governmental transparency. This and the absence of an authentic rule of law characterize illiberal democracies.

Rise of religiously motivated politics: Religiously motivated politics have appeared in predominantly Muslim, Buddhist, Hindu, Christian, and Jewish nation-states. Political groups work to make their religious values the public values of the regime and government.

Rise of nativist politics: In reaction to immigrants, asylum seekers, and growing immigrant populations, nativist political parties have gained popularity.

Growing inequalities: Increasing gaps in income and wealth between the most and least fortunate groups create doubts about the effectiveness of democracy.

Examples of democratization:

- ⚑ **UK:** Liberal democracy, new supreme court, rising popularity of the SNP and the UKIP

- ⚑ **Russia:** Illiberal democracy; Liberal Democrats and strain of xenophobia in the political culture

- ⚑ **China:** Regime seemingly impervious to democratization; politics of protest in Xinjiang and Tibet are ethnic and religious

- ⚑ **Nigeria:** Semi-liberal, elitist democracy; terrorism of Boko Haram religiously-motivated; ethnic and religious cleavages define much of the political culture

- ⚑ **Mexico:** Liberal democracy in most ways; reforms of 1990s led to electoral successes of PAN; public sentiment against Central American migrants, many of whom are heading for the US

- ⚑ **Iran:** Illiberal democracy; religiously motivated regime and politics; elections with little political import; few civil liberties or civil rights; severe limits on political activities

> SNP (Scottish National Party) is an identity politics party campaigning for Scottish independence.
>
> UKIP (UK Independence Party) is a Euro-skeptic right-wing, populist party.

DEMOCRATIZATION: WHY AND HOW?

The definition of democratization offered on p. 56 implies that regimes and governments can become less authoritarian over time. Why and how?

Authoritarian regimes fall to:

- defeat in war
- widening, deepening, or multiplying of cleavages; demographic changes
- the efforts of effective opposition either domestic, exile, or external
- diminishing state capacity
    * reduction in wealth and/or income
    * inability or unwillingness to use force as a means of social control
    * loss of legitimacy
    * large scale natural disaster
- external pressure
    * diplomatic
    * economic
    * NGO pressures and publicity
- corruption
- negative effects of economic change
- failed reforms

> Don't listen to those who speak of democracy. They all are against Islam. They want to take the nation away from its mission. – Ruhollah Khomeini, 1979

More examples of democratization:

- **UK:** Not an authoritarian regime, nonetheless discussions about proportional voting could be considered democratization.

- **Russia:** Authoritarian Soviet Union fell because of its inability to modernize and adapt to globalization. Russian governments since Yeltsin seem to have worked to create an illiberal democratic regime. Is that democratization?

- **China:** Regime seems impervious to democratization. The use of force to suppress dissent and extra-judicial "reeducation" programs are widespread.

- **Nigeria:** Elitist groups are nearly as divided by cleavages as everyone else, making authoritarianism difficult even for military governments. Domestic economic limitations (capacities) might encourage greater transparency. Corruption is endemic.

- **Mexico:** PRI semi-authoritarian dominance ended as a result of domestic economic change and electoral reforms as well as global economic pressures.

- **Iran:** The Islamic Republic was an attempt to build religious and democratic façade to Persian and Shiite authoritarian systems. Rulers with power are unlikely to allow real steps toward democratization without a motivating crisis.

POLITICAL ECONOMICS

Political stability depends to a large degree on economic stability and relative prosperity.

BASIC DEFINITIONS

Fiscal policy: government decisions about total public spending and revenue that result in budgetary deficits or surpluses

Monetary policy: policies that affect interest rates and the supply of money available within an economy

Government spending for public good and services include
- the costs of governing
- national defense
- public enterprises and infrastructure investments
- social welfare programs
- subsidies to valued economic activities

Government revenues include
- taxes and license fees
- income from public enterprises
- income from the sale of public assets (e.g., natural resources or public enterprises)
- aid from other countries and/or international organizations (e.g., IMF or World Bank)

Public spending contributes to the economy. In some countries, it dominates the economy. Since resources are finite, public spending competes with private spending especially in countries with large social welfare programs.

Public saving describes an economy in which government revenues are more than government spending. Public saving, like private saving, slows the economy. This can reduce inflation and prevent instability caused by growth that is too rapid. It can also reduce national debt and deter economic recovery from recession when public spending is too low.

Deficit spending occurs when governments spend more than they receive in revenues. This can stabilize the economy or promote growth if the economy is in recession unless the economy is overly dependent upon public spending. It can cause inflation if the economy is growing near its capacity.

Austerity describes policies to reduce public spending and revenues with the goals of reducing public debt and encouraging private sector growth.

Interest rates are increased by government policies to slow down or stabilize economic growth; rates are lowered to encourage growth. Even in market economies, governments have a great deal of influence over interest rates through direct policies and public investments.

The supply of money influences interest rates, inflation, and business activity. Governments exercise great control over the supply of money. In market economies, the lending activities of banking institutions also affect the supply of money.

National debt is the sum of deficits and surpluses in government budgets over time. It is owed to holders of government bonds (i.e., loans to the government by citizens, outside investors, and other countries).

NATIONAL DEBT AS A PERCENTAGE OF GDP
(2015 Estimates from the *CIA World Factbook*)

Iran: 11.4%	China: 22.4%
Nigeria: 11.7%	Mexico: 41.0%
Russia: 13.4%	United Kingdom: 86.6%

MEASURING ECONOMIES

GDP (Gross Domestic Product): equal to the market value of legal goods and services produced in a nation-state in a specific time period (usually a year)

GDP is the most widely used measure of the size of economies.

HDI (Human Development Index): a statistic based upon life expectancy, education, and income data from most of the world's countries

The creators of the HDI claim that combining social welfare and economic data offers more meaningful comparisons between countries than GDP does.

GDP COMPARISON	HDI COMPARISON
(2014 estimates from the *CIA World Factbook*— out of 229 countries)	(from the 2014 Human Development Report of the UNDP— out of 172 countries)
#1 China	#14 United Kingdom
#7 Russia	#57 Russia
#11 United Kingdom	#71 Mexico
#12 Mexico	#75 Iran
#19 Iran	#91 China
#21 Nigeria	#152 Nigeria

GDP per capita: takes into account the populations of the countries being compared.

Advocates of the value of this statistic suggest that it better measures the social value of a country's production.

GDP PER CAPITA COMPARISON

(2014 world rankings and estimates from the *CIA World Factbook*)

#49	UK	$37,700
#69	Russia	24,800
#92	Mexico	17,900
#96	Iran	16,500
#113	China	12,900
#159	Nigeria	6,100

Gini coefficient: accounts for income distribution

Corrado Gini invented this measure of inequality. Higher numbers indicate greater economic inequality.

GINI COEFFICIENT COMPARISON

(2014 estimates from the *CIA World Factbook*)

UK	32.3
Russia	42.0
Nigeria	43.7
Iran	44.5
China	47.3
Mexico	48.3

TYPES OF ECONOMIES

Market economy: an economic system in which supply, demand, investment, production, distribution, and prices of goods and services are primarily determined by voluntary exchanges in transparent markets

Command economy: an economic system (some are called planned economies) in which public or private policy decisions substantially substitute for markets in determining prices, production, and distribution of economic goods and services

Mixed economy: an economic system in which markets, public policy, and powerful actors all play important roles in answering the basic economic questions

Basic economic questions:

- What to produce?
- How to produce?
- For whom to produce?
- How to distribute production?

Agricultural economy: a system in which the agricultural sector employs the most people and produces most of the economic goods.

Industrial economy: a system in which the manufacturing of material goods employs the most people and produces most of the systems profits.

Post-industrial or service economy: a system in which the largest sector of the economy provides skilled, specialized, or more general services.

SECTORS OF ECONOMIES: PERCENTAGES OF TOTAL GDP

(from *CIA World Factbook*, 2012 estimates)

A: Agriculture; M: Manufacturing; S: Services

	A	M	S
UK	0.6	21	79
Russia	4	36	60
China	10	44	46
Nigeria	21	26	53
Mexico	4	36	60
Iran	9	41	50

POLITICAL AND ECONOMIC DEVELOPMENT

Political leaders want their economies and wealth to grow. Moving from an agricultural economy to an industrial economy is usually seen as the first step. Political leaders have used many tools to pursue those goals.

Nationalization: appropriating means of production from private owners or former colonizers, often after a revolution, independence, or a major crisis

Communist revolutions in Russia and China and nationalizations in the UK and Mexico are classic examples. The creation of charitable foundations (*bonyads*) from businesses seized by revolutionaries in Iran after 1979 is a variation of the theme.

Import substitution: discouraging the importation of goods and encouraging the domestic production of those goods to grow the economy

In theory, if the investment that creates the productive capacity comes from within the country or as unrestricted foreign aid, the profits will remain in the country. In reality, investors in unstable economies will export their profits as soon as possible.

Parastatals: state-owned enterprises (SOE), usually created to serve a public purpose like transport, communications, extracting natural resources, or marketing a country's goods and services

These are common tools used by countries (like Nigeria) that are wary of or have difficulty attracting investment from outside the country.

Rentier status: when a country's government (like Nigeria's) relies on the sale (rent) of natural resources for most of its revenue

Taxes are negligible and put no restraints on policy.

CHALLENGES

Globalization: the growing adoption of common values, procedures, and popular culture around the world

Globalization is seen both as a roadblock to self-directed economic development and as a means to create more growth in the long run for countries seeking to industrialize.

> **International Monetary Fund**: A self-governing organization whose goals are to promote global growth and economic stability. It offers advice and loans to resolve economic problems and instability. It also funds programs to reduce poverty.

> **World Bank**: A self-governing organization dedicated to reducing poverty by promoting international trade and foreign capital investment. Provides loans to "developing" countries for capital programs.

The IMF usually demands economic reforms that make markets more important in exchange for economic aid. **Economic liberalization, structural adjustment (austerity),** and **privatization** reforms aim to reduce the roles of government and politicians in the economic arena. They also often reduce social welfare programs.

Both institutions have insisted on austerity (government spending reductions) and privatization of parastatals in countries where they determine that national debt is too high.

Critics charge both groups with neo-colonialism.

Corruption: the illegitimate use of political or economic power for personal or illegal purposes

Corruption is a threat to political and economic stability as well as to political legitimacy and markets.

Transparency: the ability for outsiders to see and understand the negotiations, planning, and actions of political and economic actors; necessary for functioning of free markets and accountable government and politics

Affinity networks: corruption often takes place within networks that link people.

- ► **UK:** Political parties, "old boys" (groups of school and university alumni)

- ► **Russia:** Nomenklatura; *siloviki* (security services), integration of government and business

- ► **China:** *Guanxi*, Communist Party, SOEs, party supervision of private businesses

- ► **Nigeria:** Powerful ethnic identities and loyalties;

- ► **Mexico:** Camarillas; political parties, especially the PRI

- ► **Iran:** Patron-client networks in religious and business circles; charitable foundations (*bonyads*) that control much of the economy without oversight or taxation

> This [electoral] system was disastrous when the city had become corrupt. For then it was not the most virtuous but the most powerful who stood for election. — Niccolo Machiavelli

Transparency in relevant case studies:

- **UK:** Quite transparent commercial and political arenas; corruption not endemic, primarily a problem of individual crimes

- **Russia:** Bribery part of historic political culture; citizens believe elected officials, civil servants, and police are corrupt; multi-national companies are discouraged from investing; the integration of politics and business facilitates corruption

- **China:** Bribery and embezzlement endemic; the integration of politics and business facilitates corruption; rapidly growing economic inequalities result in large part from corruption

- **Nigeria:** Belief that public assets belong to those in power and the ethnic groups they lead (called *prebendalism* by some Western scholars); centralized government/political control of oil wealth; limited capacity of the state to prevent or control corruption is a factor

- **Mexico:** Corruption endemic among politicians and police; bribery and embezzlement are common; drug cartels active in buying and selling protection

- **Iran:** Smuggling is common as a way to avoid sanctions; supporters of high-ranking politicians and clerics gain access to public funds; shortages caused by sanctions resolved with bribes and smuggling

Transparency International is an NGO that evaluates and publicizes reports of corruption in business and politics. Its main publication is the Corruption Perceptions Index, a collection of reports from reputable sources. The result is a yearly ranking of how corrupt business and political systems are around the world.

The 2014 Corruption Perceptions Index ranked 176 countries. Denmark was ranked as the least corrupt country with a score of 92 out of 100.

2014 CORRUPTION PERCEPTIONS INDEX

#	Country	Score
#14	UK	78
#100	China	39
#103	Mexico	35
#136	Russia	27
#136	Iran	27
#136	Nigeria	27

Freedom House is a non-governmental organization (primarily funded by the United States) that conducts research and advocacy on democracy, political freedom, and human rights.

In 2014, the *Freedom in the World* report categorized the **United Kingdom** as **"free"** with a score of 1.

Mexico and **Nigeria** were labeled **"partly free"** with scores of 3 and 4, respectively.

Russia, **Iran**, and **China** were categorized as **"not free."** Their scores were 6, 6, and 7, respectively.

POLITICAL AND ECONOMIC CHANGE — 71

PUBLIC POLICY

Decisions made by a government that define its goals and actions are called **public policy.**

Where are public policy decisions made?

The more general and more important the policy decision, the higher the level of decision making.

Some policy decisions are made in the executive and the bureaucracy, some in the legislature, some in the judiciary, depending upon the nature of the regime.

What influences public policy decisions?
- politics within the government and the regime
- perceived needs of the society and the nation-state
- public opinion
- results of previous policies
- powerful individuals in a system
- political parties and interest groups
- international and supranational agreements and organizations
- threats to a government or a regime
- policies of other nation-states
- economic forces
- environmental factors

Public policy decisions in relevant case studies:

- ⚑ **UK:** Policy comes from parties and lobbyists who persuade government to propose and adopt positions that are shaped by the bureaucracy and adopted by Parliament.

- ⚑ **Russia:** Policy decisions are made at the highest levels of government, especially within the *siloviki* (power ministries in the president's cabinet); policy is implemented by bureaucracy, SOEs, and local government units.

- ⚑ **China:** The Standing Committee of Politburo of the Communist Party of China is the final decision making body for public policy; party and government bureaucracies, SOEs, and lower level governments implement policy.

- ⚑ **Nigeria:** Policy decisions are made by political and bureaucratic (technocratic) elite at a national level; they are implemented by national and state governments and bureaucracies.

- ⚑ **Mexico:** Policy ideas come from parties, interest groups, and technocratic elites; policies adopted by governments align with ruling party's ideas. Currently some policy ideas seem to be multi-partisan. Divided government allows the executive to be central to public policy decisions.

- ⚑ **Iran:** Policy making is not transparent. Clerical, military, economic, and technocratic elites (often unified) propose policies. Top clerical and military authorities make final decisions, which are adopted by the legislature and the government.

What public policies are most common?

- economic policies: fiscal (spending and revenue), monetary matters, economic growth and stability, inflation (see p. 60)

- national defense and foreign policies

- education

- employment

- social welfare (individual support, unemployment, health care, and pensions)

- agricultural (food production and distribution)

- natural resources

- environment and climate change

- infrastructure (transportation, communication)

- citizen participation

- individual rights and liberties

- immigration and population

- cleavages (ethnic, religious, social class, geographic, gender, age, etc.)

> Students should "explore how different systems create different solutions to domestic and global problems..."
> — AP course description

Prominent policy issues in relevant case studies:

- ⚑ **UK**: Recently economic and social welfare policies have dominated UK politics. Austerity (reducing government spending) has been a primary tool of the government; immigration is divisive.

- ⚑ **Russia**: Economic policies have been prominent. Civil society issues have been important as have individual liberties. Foreign policy decisions have been newsworthy.

- ⚑ **China**: Maintaining economic growth and modernizing infrastructure have been major goals. Maintaining Communist Party control is a big deal. Fighting a perception and the reality of massive corruption is also important.

- ⚑ **Nigeria**: Economic development and infrastructure creation (especially electricity and water) are vital. Endemic corruption is discussed, but little is done. Terrorism and opposition to the government is evident.

- ⚑ **Mexico**: Conflict with drug cartels and associated violence is front and center. Economic growth and modernization have been important enough recently to persuade parties to say they'll work together.

- ⚑ **Iran**: Economic issues (especially the sanctions) are profound, but often seem to take a back seat to nationalism. Nationalism, sovereignty, and foreign policy are important. Political participation and individual liberties are also high on some peoples' lists of priorities (but not the government's list).

What influences on public policy decisions threaten sovereignty?

- **World Trade Organization (WTO):** This transnational membership organization aims to settle trade disputes and "liberalize" international trade (i.e., remove legal barriers). Member nation-states have yet to resolve the issues of agricultural subsidies which rich nations want to preserve and poorer nations want to reduce. Settling outstanding issues would imply that most nations would have less independent control of their policies.

- **EU (European Union):** The EU is a supranational organization that assumes some of the powers (sovereignty) of member nation-states. The UK is very defensive of its sovereignty and sensitive about EU infringements on its independence (the major reason it doesn't belong to the monetary union).

- **World Bank:** The World Bank is an international organization whose goals include reducing poverty and dealing with global environmental issues. Twentieth century structural adjustment policies imposed on borrowing countries made poverty worse and took away nation-states' autonomy in making economic policies (see p. 67).

- **IMF (International Monetary Fund):** The IMF is an international organization whose goals include facilitating international economic activity. "Conditionality" of loans has often required structural adjustment, which limits nation-states' sovereignty (see p. 67).

- **NAFTA (North American Free Trade Agreement):** A multi-lateral trade treaty under which signatories cede some of their sovereignty to treaty mechanisms for dispute resolution.

- **Environmental issues:** Things like climate change, localized and general shortages of water, rapid and uneven population growth, and cross-border pollution all present nation-states with policy problems that are not amenable to isolated policy making.

- **Income distribution and taxation issues:** Globalization presents policy choices about problems like growing economic inequalities, urbanization, and differential taxation rates as things that are not amenable to independent action.

- **Global culture:** The spread of cultural memes and values (from McDonalds to soccer to fundamentalism to pop music to ideas about human rights) can bring change even if policy makers in power are opposed to it.

INTRODUCTION TO COMPARATIVE POLITICS (PART TWO)

Political science is an **empirical** discipline.

Political science's body of knowledge is derived from evidence that can be physically perceived. Logic and empirically based natural laws are used to evaluate human perceptions. It's a social science.

Ideals and ideologies are not empirical. They are **normative**.

They do, however, motivate political action and become the province for study by political scientists. Ideals and ideology often motivate political study as well.

> It's especially true in comparative politics that ideas about what is (or should be) normal (normative) motivate attempts to describe which political systems or behaviors are more functional (a normative judgment), efficient (possibly an empirical judgment), powerful (a normative and/or an empirical judgment), or desirable (a normative judgment).

"Show us the facts," say the empiricists.

"Show us what's good," say the idealists.

Some political scientists do their research by measuring, counting things, and statistically analyzing the results. They're identified as **quantitative** investigators.

Others observe things less amenable to numerical measurement, like patriotism. They do **qualitative** research.

Most political scientists use **both** quantitative and qualitative methods.

The Communist Party of China "must... consolidate confidence in socialism with Chinese characteristics," Chinese President Xi Jinping said. (Xinhua, 26 June 2013)

Is Xi an idealist or empiricist?

President Xi Jinping and President Enrique Peña Nieto exchange toasts in Mexico City in 2013 after signing agreements to broaden relations between their countries and expand their trade ties

ANSWER: Since Xi is talking about a normative goal ("socialism with Chinese characteristics"), he is an idealist.

Political scientists look for **patterns** or **correlations** between independent and dependent variables. The goal is to make valid **generalizations**.

When comparing cases, political scientists often design research that looks for

- significant differences between two or more very similar cases (**Most Similar Systems** or **MSS** research designs), e.g., What causes the differences between two formerly Communist countries like Russia and China?

  or

- significant similarities between two or more very different cases (**Most Different Systems** or **MDS** research designs), e.g., Why do the political cultures in the UK and Iran apparently value representative government?

Thanks to John Stuart Mill for those ideas!

Case studies might be examples of regimes, governments, states, nation-states, political cultures, electoral systems, judicial systems, bureaucracies, political party systems, recruitment methods, systems of socialization, etc.

When doing comparative research, political scientists must identify and analyze:

Constants: any of those things in comparative case analysis that are essentially identical in the examples studied

Correlations: apparent associations between variables

Independent variables: any of the inputs, institutions, or processes that shape the results of government decision and/or policy making

Dependent variables: results of political decisions and actions, which are determined by the inputs, institutions, and processes (the independent variables)

Intervening variables: factors influenced by independent variables that affect changes in a dependent variable

Causations: correlations in which a change in one variable results in change in others

Multiple causality: the simultaneous effects of a number of independent and intervening variables that bring about changes in dependent variables

And they must be careful to avoid:

Reductivism: attempts to explain complex correlations and causations using a single independent variable; oversimplification

COMPARATIVE THEORIES

Theoretical approaches tell researchers what "things" to look at and how to understand what they observe.

Systems Theory: assumes comparative studies should focus on the inputs to and products (policies and actions) of political systems and their environments to explain political behavior

Since inputs to a political system, environments outside a political system, and feedback from previous policy decisions and actions influence new policy-making, all aspects need to be considered.

Rational Choice Theory: assumes that people act rationally in their own self-interests and that understanding their perceptions will explain their behavior. Therefore comparative studies should focus on individual behavior and motivation.

Structural Theory: assumes that human behavior is guided by underlying social, political, and economic arrangements. Understanding the basic structures of society will explain political behavior. Therefore comparative studies should focus on structures and relationships.

Cultural Theory: assumes that people who share a common identity also share ways of believing and behaving. Understanding these beliefs and the motives for behaviors (and their evolution) will explain political behavior. Therefore comparative studies should focus on the cultural contexts within which people act politically.

Political scientists often interpret their observations through multiple theoretical lenses.

All political systems face similar issues. The methods of dealing with those issues differ widely and that opens the door to comparative studies.

- **Environmental issues**: Clean air, clean water, and adequate arable land are necessities.

- **Economic issues**: Political systems are inextricably involved in production and distribution of economic goods.

- **Diversity**: Cleavages between ethnic or social groups create disunity.

- **Social welfare**: Public health, health care, support for those unable to care for themselves, emergency aid for victims of disaster are all important for social stability.

- **Justice**: Even an authoritarian system, unless it relies on overwhelming force, needs to be seen as fair.

- **Self-protection**: A political system must preserve its own existence and sovereignty.

Aristotle (in *Politics*) compared political systems based on how many "rulers" there were and whether policies benefited the society in general or just the rulers.

What theoretical approach was Aristotle using?

ANSWER: Aristotle's approach was a structural one.

CASE STUDIES

The final part of the course description identifies the case studies that you will be tested upon.

Course description: "Six countries form the core of the AP Comparative Government and Politics course: China, Great Britain, Iran, Mexico, Nigeria, and Russia."

"Students successfully completing this course will:

- **understand** major comparative political concepts, themes, and generalizations
- **have knowledge** of important facts pertaining to the governments and politics of China, Great Britain, Iran, Mexico, Nigeria, and Russia
- **understand** typical patterns of political processes and behavior and their consequences
- **be able to compare and contrast** political institutions and processes across countries and to derive generalizations
- **be able to analyze and interpret** basic data relevant to comparative government and politics"

(Emphasis added by author. – KW)

In the 55 multiple choice questions (MCQs) and eight free response questions (FRQs) on the AP exam, you'll be asked to demonstrate your **knowledge** and your **understanding** of the ideas outlined in the earlier pages of this book.

You will be tested on the **facts** about the government and politics of the "six countries" that "form the core" of the course.

You will be asked to **assess the results** of "typical... political processes and ... behaviors..."

You will be asked to **create or evaluate** generalizations based on examples from the "six countries."

You will have to show that you **understand basic data** and are able to **communicate** that understanding to others.

> Remember: MCQs ask for the "best" not the right answer. No DBQs (document-based questions) on this exam. Some of the FRQs are short answer questions; others demand greater exposition. **Follow the instructions.**

THE UNITED KINGDOM

The UK is one of the richest and most powerful countries in the world. It has a very long tradition of **rule of law**. It's had a broadly **representative** system of government since the first half of the 19th century, although women didn't get to vote until 1918.

The territory is relatively small by global standards, but its population of 63 million people is the 22nd largest in the world. Over 80% of the people live in cities and over 90% are white. The population is growing slowly. Estimates are that 99% of the people are literate.

POLITICAL CULTURE

The political culture is vital because widely shared values (like fairness and transparency) and traditions (like rule of law and *stare decisis*) take the place of a written constitution.

Things like representative government and fair trials are considered normal and necessary. In spite of the existence of a state church (Church of England), separation of church and politics has been an important principle for centuries.

CLEAVAGES

The social class cleavage is large, and economic inequality has increased in the past decade. Nationalism, a shared political culture, and extensive social welfare programs diminish the divisions. The values of *noblesse oblige* (duty to society) and deference (respect for superiors) also help to bridge class cleavages and promote political unity. Major parties are able to win votes across class differences.

A notable geographic-economic cleavage between the south of England and the north of England, Scotland, and Wales is troublesome. Wealth and high tech industry is centered in the south. Labour still earns more votes than other parties outside of southern England.

The cleavages between Catholics (mostly Irish) and Protestants (mostly Scottish and English) persist in Northern Ireland. Things are much less violent than they were before the Good Friday Agreement in 1998.

Divisions between the English, the Scots, and the Welsh continue, especially the one between the Scots and the English. Devolution, intended to reduce the political significance of that national cleavage, has instead whetted the appetites of Scots for self-rule. After losing a referendum on independence, the Scottish National Party (SNP) has risen to a position of political power, winning 59 seats in the 2015 election. The rise of the SNP has reduced the power of Labour.

CIVIL SOCIETY

Civil society is free and active in the UK. Local groups are organized for self-help schemes and issue advocacy. Many citizens are active in international NGOs. Religious organizations are unrestricted, but only about 20% of people are active in them.

REGIME

In this parliamentary system, political power is held by a government that is part of the legislature. The Prime Minister is **head of government** (p. 6) and the leader of the majority party or coalition in the legislature. Nearly all the members of the **government** (cabinet, p. 32) are members of Parliament, and each heads a government ministry.

Ultimate executive, legislative and judicial power was **fused** (p. 28) in the **legislature** until 2009, when a separate supreme court was established to meet the demands of **EU** treaties.

One part of the bicameral parliament is the House of Lords, whose members are mostly appointed by the monarch as instructed by the government. A few seats are hereditary. It has little power.

Real power resides in the House of Commons, from which the **government** is chosen by majority vote. There are currently 650 seats in Commons. Members of parliament (MPs) are elected from **single member districts** in **plurality elections**. Parliamentary elections take place every five years.

The system is **unitary**. Political power for the whole country resides in the government. Limited powers have been granted to national legislatures in Scotland, Wales, and Northern Ireland in a process called **devolution**. Even more limited powers are granted to county and city councils to administer local services.

The government **executive** includes a large and powerful **bureaucracy**. While government ministers head each ministry, the expertise and experience of the bureaucrats makes them very influential.

The **judiciary** is made up of the Supreme Court and a hierarchy of lower courts. Defendants can appeal lower court decisions. Judicial systems in Scotland, Wales, and Northern Ireland include features unique to each national **political culture**. Judges are selected by independent committees and appointed by the monarch as instructed by the government. There is a high degree of respect for the law and the judiciary.

PARTIES

There are two major political parties:

- **Conservative (Tory) Party**—Current Prime Minister (head of government, p. 6) David Cameron is head of the party.

- **Labour Party**—The leader of the largest minority party leads the "opposition" and is head of the "shadow cabinet," which tracks and publicizes policies and actions of the government.

There are a number of minority parties as well:

- In 2015, the Scottish National Party became the third largest party in Commons. It won all its seats from Labour. Its main goals are preserving Scotland's social welfare system and independence for Scotland.

- There are nationalist parties in Wales and Northern Ireland. The United Kingdom Independence Party (UKIP) is the best known of the extremist parties. It elected one MP in 2015.

- The **Liberal Democratic Party** has been around as a minority third party for a long time. In the 2015 election, LDP lost nearly all of its seats in the House of Commons.

The largest parties try to be "**catch-all**" parties that win votes from a wide spectrum of citizens.

The **Conservative Party** is a center-right party; the **Liberal Democrats** try to be a centrist party; and the **Labour Party** is a center-left party.

Contested policies focus on economic and welfare state issues. **Conservatives** generally argue in favor of privatization of public services, greater efficiencies in government programs, less regulation and taxation. The party is badly split on the role of the UK in the EU. Many Tories are opposed to membership.

The **Labour Party** opposes many privatization suggestions; it supports efforts at greater efficiencies in public programs but wants to guarantee that public services and support are provided to all who need them. Regulation and taxation are seen as necessary for the national good. The party supports EU membership and many support joining the Monetary Union.

INTEREST GROUPS

The most powerful nationwide interest groups are economic organizations:

- Confederation of British Industry
- Trades Union Congress
- National Farmers Union
- British Medical Association.

Groups that advocate on environmental and human rights issues are often related to international NGOs like Greenpeace, Friends of the Earth, Oxfam, and Amnesty International.

Lobbying is done at high levels of party and government. "Back benchers" (legislators who are not part of the government or the loyal opposition shadow cabinet) are normally not lobbied except on very local issues.

MEDIA

Published media in the UK are national, rather than regional. Tabloid newspapers are the most popular but tend to sensationalize news and focus on celebrities. "Quality" publications have well-known biases and are considered reliable sources.

The BBC and its commercial partners dominate broadcast media. News reporting is considered excellent. Satellite and cable systems offer alternatives to the independent broadcasters and the government-owned BBC system.

Communications are facilitated by 33 million telephone landlines and 82 million cell phones. Over 8 million Internet hosts serve the needs of an estimated 51 million Internet users.

ECONOMY

The UK's GDP of $2.4 trillion makes it the 11th largest economy in the world. The per capita GDP ($37,700 in 2014) ranked 44th in the world.

In 2012 the government collected about 40% of the GDP in taxes. Largest taxes are income tax, national insurance tax (retirement, unemployment, and health insurance), value added tax (sales tax), and corporate income tax.

Military spending was 2.5% of GDP. The government deficit (p. 61) was nearly $5 billion in 2014.

RECRUITMENT

Politically ambitious citizens get involved in local party organizations as soon as possible and work their way up. Oxford and Cambridge degrees and (in the Labour Party) union leadership experience are big assets for the very top jobs.

Inexperienced candidates are nominated for parliamentary seats that parties do not expect to win (there is no residency requirement). More veteran party members will be nominated to run in constituencies where they have better chances of being elected. Top party leaders run in districts they are sure to win.

RUSSIA

The Russian tradition of authoritarianism is as long as the British rule of law tradition. There is not a tradition of representative government in this military and economic super power. The political turmoil of the past 150 years continues.

Russia is geographically the world's largest nation by far. Its population of 142 million ranks it in the top ten. About 74% of the people live in cities and 80% of the people are Russians. Small, geographically centered minorities live on the southern and eastern border areas. Over 99% of the population is literate. The population is shrinking.

POLITICAL CULTURE

Surprisingly, given the huge size of the country, political culture is much the same across the continent. Part of the reason for this is the long history of Tsarist and Soviet rule and efforts to encourage westward migration and the Russification* of the frontiers.

There are also small centers of local political power that are in practice more independent of policies and practices of the national government.

Public opinion polls show support for free elections, individual liberties, and strong, stable leadership. These values dominate the political culture along with powerful

---

*   Russification: Tsarist, Soviet, and Russian policies to encourage ethnic Russians to migrate to areas dominated by non-Russian ethnic groups and to the promotion of Russian language, culture, and politics in non-Russian areas like the Baltics and central Asia; similar to Chinese policies for the Sinofication of areas like Tibet and Xinjiang

Russification is what christian people do but w/ culture instead of religion nationalism (among the Russians). The result is an **illiberal democracy** where obedience and stability are highly valued.

CLEAVAGES

Social class and ethnicity define the biggest cleavages. A tiny rich elite and a small middle class are separated from massive underclasses. Energy sales have provided some money for wages for public employees and social welfare, but poverty is widespread, especially in rural areas.

Scattered small ethnic groups on the periphery of the country are divided from most Russians by nationality, geography, and religion. The wars in Chechnya are extreme examples of conflict resulting from the cleavages.

CIVIL SOCIETY

Civil society in Russia has never been a big force. It began growing in the last decade of the 20th century, but the government has attempted to prevent independent groups from exercising political power recently. Russian organizations have been prohibited from getting support from international NGOs. Independent groups have been investigated and had their offices closed (e.g., Moscow Helsinki Group). Even individual protests (e.g., Pussy Riot) have been suppressed.

popular band that speak out on certain political issues

Religious organizations have had greater freedom in the last 20 years as long as they support the government or avoid politics. The Russian Orthodox Church has been closely allied with Putin's governments. Anti-government activity or statements by religious authorities or congregants are often suppressed.

no separation of church & state

REGIME

While the regime resembles a representative system structurally, it functions as an **illiberal democracy**. While formally a federation, it functions more like a **unitary** system.

unitary vs. illiberal democracy

The **head of state** is the president, chosen for a six-year term in a majority (two-round) election. The **head of government** is the premier, appointed by the president and confirmed by the lower house of the legislature.

Both the president and the premier have **cabinets**. The ministers in the premier's cabinet, who are heads of government ministries, are appointed by the president. A Presidential Administration (executive office) and a Security Council report directly to and serve the president. The Security Council is made up of the power ministries and the premier. Bureaucrats hired by all these executive agencies are chosen for their loyalty to the president and the regime.

Since Russia's seizure of Crimea and the imposition of economic sanctions on Russia, President Putin has taken steps to strengthen the powers of the presidency and its Security Council. More and more social policy, economic, and foreign policy decisions are being made of the highest levels of the executive.

The **legislature** is made up of the **State Duma** and the **Federation Council**. The Duma has 450 members who are elected in **proportional (party list)** elections every four years. The Federation Council is made up of 166 members appointed by executive and legislative officials in 83 members of the federation.

The top of the **judiciary** consists of the:

- Supreme Court
- Constitutional Court
- Superior Court of Arbitration

All judges are nominated by the president and appointed by the Federation Council. Below these courts are republic, regional, and provincial courts from which appeals can be made to higher courts.

PARTIES

There's really only one party that matters, **United Russia**. It's the creation of Putin and his allies, and it has dominated Russian politics for the last decade. Until recently it ran a youth organization called Nashi to recruit aspiring leaders and keep them enthused. Nashi ran workshops to train political activists, organized demonstrations to support government policies, and held summer camps for loyalists.

The Communist Party is still around and organized nationally. It attracts votes from socialists and people who long for the social welfare programs and prestige of the Soviet Union. The Liberal Democratic Party is a misnamed **nativist** party that campaigns against non-Russians and democratic government. There are other parties that are authentically democratic, both **center right** and **center left**, but they don't win many votes.

United Russia's leaders have even created faux parties at election time to compete with weaker rivals, for instance a United Russia-sponsored party that advocates "Russia first" policies like the Liberal Democrats. This takes votes away from them and reduces the chance that Liberal Democratic candidates can win any seats in the Duma. United Russia is a vehicle for Putin's power base and pursues nationalistic policies that strengthen the country, its economy, and the party's power.

INTEREST GROUPS

The most influential forces in the Russian state are essentially integrated into the government. SOEs and the oligarchs who control the largest energy companies find it easy to make their preferences known because of their close associations with the politically powerful.

Until recently, Russian "chapters" of international **NGOs** like Greenpeace, Human Rights Watch, Amnesty International, and World Wildlife Fund (see p. 47) were actively lobbying the government. In the last three years, the government has passed laws that cut off the Russian organizations from outside support and crippled their operations.

Groups generally supportive of government policy operate more freely. The Russian Orthodox Church, for example, has won great policy and financial support.

Most lobbying is done at high levels within the government and United Russia.

MEDIA

While large segments of the print and broadcast media are privately owned, owners are closely associated with Putin and United Russia. One of the main vehicles for this is Gazprom, the world's largest producer of natural gas. It owns, as subsidiaries, television networks, a satellite television service, radio networks, magazine and book publishing companies, a film production company, a chain of movie theaters, Internet hosts, advertising agencies, and a real estate management company. All seem to be at the service of the government. Public opinion polls show that people recognize the biases of the reporting but believe that is acceptable. Other companies own and control other parts of the media.

Most newspapers are regional, not national. Owners of the most-read newspapers are also associated with the government. All of the largest news agencies are government-owned. Freedom of the press is passively restrained.

In a huge country, the 43 million telephone lines and 262 million cell phones are important for communications. Telephone companies are privately owned but publicly regulated. The same is true for the 15 million Internet hosts, which serve 41 million users.

ECONOMY

Russia produced (GDP) $3.6 trillion worth of goods and services in 2014. That made it the 7th largest economy in the world. Unlike much of Europe, the economy was growing very slowly in 2014. Per capita GDP was $124,800 (69th in the world), but great inequalities mean that it's difficult to evaluate general prosperity.

Government revenues in 2014 totaled $416 billion (about 20% of GDP). Primary sources of revenue are the Value Added Tax, a levy on natural resource extraction, corporate profits tax, a tax on alcoholic beverages, a "Unified Social Tax" (to pay for retirements and medical insurance), and a personal income tax.

Public spending was $408 billion, meaning there was surplus spending of about $8 billion. Military spending was $126 billion, 3.5% of GDP.

RECRUITMENT

Loyalty and activism are essential qualifications for anyone seeking to secure a position of power. Those qualities can be demonstrated within United Russia, a government ministry (especially one of the security ministries), or a SOE. People in positions of power are looking for protégés.

THE PEOPLE'S REPUBLIC OF CHINA (PRC)

China is the most populous country on earth. The PRC's authoritarian regime is heir to at least two thousand years of authoritarian tradition. The civilization was overwhelmed in the 19th century because the inertia of its own traditions and technological advances made in Europe.

China is a large country (4th largest), but its population is many times that of other large countries, except India.

Today, half the huge population is urban and a middle class is growing and making demands on the government. Nearly 80% of the population lives in the eastern third of the country, making urban issues, like transportation, vital. The poverty and physical isolation of the rural half of the population stimulates even more demands on government.

POLITICAL CULTURE

Traditionally, the regime has been a unitary one and the central government has always been the organizer and motive force for public works, investment, and commerce. Historically, the individual has been seen as a contributor to society, not as a beneficiary of society's protection and success.

Anti-colonial rebellions, revolutions, and civil wars of the 20th century resulted in the creation of a Communist state modeled on Marxist ideas. Fifty years later, technocrats and advocates of economic development have consolidated their hold on political power.

CLEAVAGES

Over 90% of the people are Han Chinese. The major minorities are Tibetans and Uighurs who live in the far west of the country. These are the places of greatest civil unrest and resistance to the government. Public policy encourages Han migration to these areas and to make them more "Chinese."

The major cleavage is the urban-rural one. Urban residents have great advantages in income, education, and health care. Government-issued residential permits restrict legal migration, and illegal migrants suffer the same disadvantages as rural residents.

Secondarily, there is a massive gap between the small middle class and the smaller group of incredibly rich Chinese. Government policy aims to improve incomes and standards of living in rural areas and recently moves have been made to make rural to urban migration easier.

CIVIL SOCIETY

There is no independent civil society in the PRC. The Communist Party (CPC) makes great efforts to ensure that it controls all organized activity. Organizers of independent political activity risk arrest and re-education camp or prison sentences.

REGIME

Democratic centralism is the dominant concept describing the **unitary** Chinese regime. In theory, CPC members are to communicate to their superiors the desires and needs of the people. At the top of the system, where individuals are both party and government leaders, the popular will is distilled into workable public policies that are presented to the government for approval and implementation.

The executive is headed by the president, who is head of state. The premier is the head of government. The president is elected by National People's Congress (NPC). The premier is nominated by the president and confirmed by the NPC.

There is an administrative cabinet made up of ministers who head government ministries and who are CPC officials.

Just below the highest levels, ministers and other top bureaucrats are selected more for their loyalty to the party and government leaders. Lower in the hierarchy, government bureaucrats are well-educated experts and technocrats. There is a CPC bureaucracy that parallels the government organization. Its job is to oversee government workers and evaluate their performance.

The legislature is the unicameral National People's Congress (NPC). Its nearly 3000 delegates meet yearly to discuss and approve laws and policies proposed by their leaders and the executive. Delegates are elected by local congresses and branches of the Peoples Liberation Army (PLA).

The legislative leaders, when the NPC is not in session, are on the **NPC Central Committee** (±200 members who meet every couple months). That committee's **Standing Committee**, an even smaller group that meets more often, makes all significant policy proposals. Decisions made by these smaller groups are considered and approved by the NPC at its yearly meeting.

Like the parallel CPC bureaucracy, there is a set of parallel party legislatures, headed by the **National Party Congress**. At the top of the party system is the **CPC Central Committee** and its small elites, the **Politburo** and its **Standing Committee**.

The Politburo's Standing Committee is the actual height of political power in the PRC.

The government president is the head of the Standing Committee and the premier is the second most powerful member. It actually functions as the executive committee for the country.

The Supreme People's Court is the top of the judicial system. There are over 300 judges organized into functional tribunals (e.g., criminal, civil, and administrative jurisdictions). The chief justice is appointed for a limited term by the NPC. The chief justice nominates other judges who are approved by the NPC. Decisions by lower courts, organized by function and geography, can be appealed to higher courts.

PARTIES

While there are eight officially recognized parties outside of the Communist Party of China, the CPC is the only one with any semblance of political power.

INTEREST GROUPS

There are no recognized interest groups in China, but local officials, leaders of SOEs, and military leaders have access to Politburo members that they use to promote their policy preferences. Owners of private businesses seek similar access, many joining the CPC for that reason.

MEDIA

There is no independent media in China. There is a huge number of newspapers and magazines, but they are all published by government, party, or military organizations. Similarly, the 3,240 television channels are all run by the government, the party, or the military. Imported programming must be approved before broadcast and foreign news reporting is allowed only under strict limitations.

There are more telephones in use in China than in any other country. Almost 300 million phone lines and over a billion cell phones are used. There are nearly 400 million Internet users in the country, served by over 20 million Internet hosts. The government employs thousands of people to monitor Internet activity and to add socially acceptable content to chat rooms and Twitter-like exchanges. Internet traffic with sources outside of China is controlled by the government in the attempt to prevent Chinese citizens from seeing outside sources of information. Many people use techniques like virtual private networks (VPNs) to get around these limitations.

ECONOMY

China's GDP is over $17 trillion. It's now the largest GDP in the world. The economy has been growing faster than most others for the past decade.

The per capita GDP is estimated at $12,900 (113th in the world). That figure has also been growing more rapidly than in most other countries.

Taxes and other revenues made up just over 22% of the GDP, but that figure is misleading because of the SOEs' (p. 66) and government's nearly unlimited access to loans from government-owned banks. VAT, natural resource exploitation fees, business income taxes, and SOE surpluses are the most important sources of revenue. Officially, in 2012, the government deficit was about 3.0% of GDP.

Military spending was about 2.0% of GDP in 2012.

RECRUITMENT

CPC cadres assigned to schools try to identify ambitious and loyal citizens as early as lower school. Other cadres assigned to factories, universities, and army units identify older young people as candidates for party membership.

People who maintain good records as leaders and volunteers through their schooling and early careers are encouraged to join the CPC. Even entrepreneurs seek to join the party. It usually requires a patron to join at that point. Having a successful patron is the key to political advancement, but loyalty and enthusiasm for reaching party goals must be evident.

It's estimated that about 5% of the population are CPC members.

NIGERIA

Nigeria is the most populous of African countries. It was created in 1960 after a long, mostly non-violent political struggle for independence from the UK. Large oil reserves have made it one of the wealthiest and most powerful countries on its continent.

Its rapidly growing population, estimated at 177 million, is already the 7th largest in the world. About half the population is urban. There are over 400 ethnic/linguistic groups in Nigeria, which helps explain why only 61% can read and write. The literacy rate for men is almost 50% greater than the rate for women.

POLITICAL CULTURE

The political culture varies across the country. It includes elements of British political culture — democratic as well as authoritarian — and Islamic authoritarianism and traditions from indigenous cultures. Public opinion polls show that there is strong support for representative government and transparency, but even greater support for stability. Some leaders have worked to integrate these disparate elements, others have struggled to impose their own preferences on the whole county.

Various groups from within the military have governed the country for nearly half of the time since independence, and some of the former military leaders, like President Buhari, remain powerful political players.

There have been four consecutive civilian presidents and five general elections in the current regime, the longest span of civilian rule in Nigeria's history. The election of Buhari was the first peaceful transfer of power from one civilian political party to another.

CLEAVAGES

The divisions between groups of Nigerians are imposing. Ethnic cleavages roughly coincide with religious and geographic cleavages. Three major ethnic groups dominate the other 400. Smaller groups seek to align themselves with the larger groups.

- Hausa-Fulani: Muslim groups which dominate the northern half of the country

- Yoruba: Yoruba-speaking groups, split between Muslim, Christian, and indigenous religions, dominate the southwestern third of the country (including the largest city, Lagos)

- Igbo: mostly Christian groups who live primarily in the southeastern, oil-producing parts of the country

Larger cities throughout the country include people from all groups, most of whom live in neighborhoods segregated by ethnicity and religion.

Violent conflicts take place when events aggravate prejudices. A terrorist group in the north, Boko Haram, fights for the imposition of an Islamic state. Other violent conflicts occur in the middle of the country when Muslim herders from the north move south seeking more abundant pastures for their animals and better opportunities for themselves.

There is also a significant cleavage between the educated, English-speaking, wealthy elite and those who are not so privileged.

CIVIL SOCIETY

Civil society in Nigeria is open and free. For most people it is centered around ethnic identity and religion. If they live in the place where they were born, people are surrounded by others of their ethnicity and religion. If they have migrated to a city, they probably belong to a support group and a church or mosque connected to their ethnic identity. Ethnic groups extend to émigrés who are members of Hausa, Fulani, Yorba, Igbo, and other groups in countries to which they have emigrated.

For the elite, there are private clubs and professional organizations. Soldiers and veterans belong to military support groups. Similarly, people who have served in the National Youth Service Corps are affiliated with other "corpers" near their residences after their service.

REGIME

The regime is a federal one. A national government and 36 state governments share political power, but states are dependent upon the national government for most of their revenue.

The president is head of state and head of government, elected every four years by a majority of voters. The election might be a two-round poll if no one wins in the first ballot. A successful candidate in the first round of voting must win a majority of votes cast and at least 25% of the votes cast in two-thirds of Nigeria's states. If no candidate wins in the first round, a second round of voting pits the top two popular vote winners against one another.

The president's power is unrivaled in the regime. He appoints a cabinet to direct government ministries, receives all government oil revenues and distributes some to the states as directed by law, and commands the armed forces. The president can veto laws passed by the legislature.

The bicameral legislature consists of a Senate and a House of Representatives. Three senators are elected from districts within each state and one is elected from the Federal Capital Territory of Abuja. Three hundred-sixty representatives are elected from approximately equal population districts to the House of Representatives. As with the president, candidates must win a majority of votes cast to be elected. A second round of voting is held if no one wins a majority in the first round. The legislature enacts all laws for the country and can override presidential vetoes.

The national and state bureaucracies are large. About half of all non-agricultural jobs in Nigeria are public positions (government bureaucracy and parastatal workers). Having the right patron is key to getting government jobs.

The Supreme Court consists of 15 judges recommended by the National Judicial Council, appointed by the president, and confirmed by the Senate. There are lower courts from which appeals can be made. There is also a Sharia Court of Appeal to which Sharia court decisions can be appealed, since nearly a third of Nigeria's states have adopted Sharia law for their Muslim citizens.

PARTIES

The People's Democratic Party (PDP) dominated national politics in the Fourth Republic until 2015. Its leaders constructed and held together a coalition of northern and Yoruba politicians, current and former military leaders, and smaller ethnic groups in the middle of the country.

However, in 2013, three opposition parties merged to form the All Progressive Congress for the purpose of challenging the PDP in the elections of 2015. The APC not only won the presidency but majorities in the legislature as well. A major reason for APC success was a "feeling" by many people that it was a northerner's "turn" to be president. However, the new APC coalition is not stable. Shortly after President Buhari was sworn in, the Senate and the House elected leaders belong to the PDP.

INTEREST GROUPS

Most interest groups reflect the concerns of the educated elite. Legal professionals, physicians, and educators have active and nationwide organizations that work to influence public policy. They lobby state and national legislators, bureaucrats, and party leaders. But the most successful lobbyists are those who are in positions of power in a government or a party.

MEDIA

English language newspapers and magazines dominate print media. They are published in the largest cities, their readers are the educated elite, and their circulations are relatively small.

Parastatals run by the national and state governments operate over 100 television stations. There are also privately owned television stations, cable, and satellite services available in larger cities.

The national and state governments also run radio stations across the country that compete with private broadcasters. These stations gain political influence by broadcasting in local languages or pidgin that is understood by most people.

Cell phone service has overtaken landline service as an important tool. The 113 million cell phones vastly outnumber the 418,000 wired phones. Nigeria, in 2009, had an estimated 44 million Internet users, served by 1,200 Internet hosts. However, in 2010, a new Internet cable linking West Africa and Europe was activated. Internet usage has likely grown since then, but it has not been recorded.

ECONOMY

Nigeria's GDP is over $1 trillion, making it the 21st largest economy in the world. Oil sales account for about 10% of that GDP, but make up 80% of government income. The economy is growing nearly as rapidly as China's.

The GDP per capita is $6,100 (159th in the world). Nearly 70% of the people live below Nigeria's poverty line, and the percentage has been rising in the last decade.

Because oil sales produce most government revenue, taxes make up only 3.8% of GDP. A VAT, corporate and personal income taxes are imposed. Public spending in 2014 totaled $23 billion. The budget deficit for that year was about 2% of GDP.

RECRUITMENT

People in positions of power at the national level seek clients who will support them and in turn offer them access to the power and money associated with public office. Usually, they seek people who belong to their own ethnic group, but more and more, in the Fourth Republic, patrons seek a diverse group of clients. Ambitious politicians, in turn, seek patrons who can help them reach positions of power. At the state level, diversity is much less of an issue except in the largest cities and in some of states in the middle of the country.

MEXICO

Mexico is a country of more than 120 million people that borders on the USA. It has long coastlines on the Pacific Ocean and the Gulf of Mexico. Its oil and mineral wealth has provided a base for industrialization, especially in the north.

Three-fourths of the people live in cities (almost 21 million in the capital city). It has the most unequal of income distributions of the countries included in this curriculum.

POLITICAL CULTURE

Its long cultural history is a point of pride as is its revolutionary tradition. Electoral politics have been a valued feature of the political system for a long time. So has corruption. The PRI (p. 111) has been the dominant political party for over 70 years. Its leaders have ruled Mexico for nearly all that time.

Mexicans hold political values that emphasize legal equality, representative government, strong, stable government, and national sovereignty. The regime has been highly centralized in spite of federalism.

Patron-client networks are powerful forces in Mexico. Patrons assemble large groups of loyal followers as they work their way up in the system. It's not unusual for there to be a very large turnover in government jobs when a patron is promoted (or elected) to a new position.

Organized crime has become a major factor in Mexico as well-organized cartels compete for territory and drug markets in the USA.

CLEAVAGES

Most people are described as mestizo, and 30% are described as Amerindian. About 9% of the population is classified as white. The white population is richer, better educated, and more likely to be in executive and power positions. However, the PRI and the electoral process encourage white and mestizo people to work together, bridging the divisions. The Amerindians live primarily in the south, are the poorest group, and the least politically active. Nationalism encourages unity.

CIVIL SOCIETY

Political parties are the primary civil society organizations in urban Mexico. They sponsor sports clubs, youth activities, and celebrations for communities.

Because of the anti-clerical aspect of the PRI and the 1910-1917 revolution, the Catholic Church has not played a major political role in civil society. The growth of Protestant churches in recent decades demonstrates the openness of the civil society.

Professional and affinity organizations are common and especially active in Mexico City. Unions associated with the PRI are common and powerful.

REGIME

Mexico is a federal republic with a very strong central government. The constitution created three branches of government with a division of powers and guarantees of civil rights. Because of the domination by PRI politicians and the power of the presidency, it has functioned much like a unitary parliamentary system. States have governors and legislatures, but less power than the national government.

The national legislature is bicameral: a Senate with 128 seats and a Chamber of Deputies with 500 seats. Legislative elections are a combination of direct, plurality votes and proportional votes (see p. 43).

Elections are run by an independent *Instituto Federal Electoral*, which was created in 1990 as part of reforms meant to give elections more legitimacy. It has been successful.

Nearly all elected officials are limited to single terms in office.

The judicial system is composed of a hierarchy of state and federal courts. The system operates mostly on a Napoleonic model, i.e., inquisitorial, statute-based system. While the Supreme Court can declare laws and government actions unconstitutional, it rarely makes rulings unfriendly to the president.

PARTIES

The *Partido Revolucionario Institucional* (PRI) has dominated Mexican politics since its formation in 1929. The PRI has held the presidency and the majority of legislative seats since then except for a few years at the beginning of the 21st century. The party has been successful because of corruption, pragmatism, and because it sought to hold power and provide benefits to the groups and networks that supported it. The mid-term elections of 2015 reduced PRI power in the legislature, but in coalition with allies it maintains majority control.

Partido Accion Nacional (PAN) is an economically and socially conservative party that held the presidency from 2000 to 2012. The center of its support is in the northwestern part of Mexico. It is not anti-clerical and many of its supporters are active Catholics. It's associated with big business interests.

The *Partido de la Revolucion Democratica* (PRD) was created by left wing leaders of the PRI. It's centered in southern and central Mexico, especially in the capital city. There's more potential than power in the organization, which has been divided by leaders' rivalries.

Partido Verde Ecologista de Mexico (PVEM) aligned with PAN to elect Vicente Fox in 2000. It aligned with the PRI in 2015. It is a minor force in Mexican politics, as are two smaller parties.

INTEREST GROUPS

Interest group lobbying is dominated by business groups. National groups representing a variety of corporate interests lobby within the PRI and other parties and in the executive branch.

Unions are also powerful interests and are often integrated into the PRI.

MEDIA

Mass media have been associated with the PRI. Favored newspapers received newsprint from the government monopoly and reporters received gifts.

Broadcast television is dominated by networks owned by two large corporations, both linked to the PRI. However, cable systems offer real competition in major cities, especially because they offer Internet access.

There are only 20 million telephone landlines, but there are over 100 million cell phones in use. There are about 16 million Internet hosts and 31 million Internet users.

ECONOMY

The free market system is dominated in some sectors by parastatals. In the past 12 years, there have been growing opportunities for private investments.

The GDP for 2014 was $2.1 trillion, making Mexico's the 12th largest economy in the world. It was growing at a 2.4% rate.

The per capita GDP was $17,900, ranking Mexico at 92nd of 229 countries. However, it is estimated that 52% of the people live below the Mexican poverty line. According to income distribution figures, Mexico has the 24th most unequal distribution in the world.

Public spending was $300 billion, or about 23% of GDP. The budget deficit in 2014 was 3.7% of GDP.

RECRUITMENT

Because of the domination of patron-client networks in Mexican politics, politically ambitious people seek to become active and valuable to a local network. Similarly, workers who become active in their unions can rise to positions of political influence.

The top positions in parties, government, and bureaucracy often go to highly educated people with technical or managerial skills. Degrees from the Universidad Nacional Autónoma de México (UNAM) in a technical field are assets. Undergraduate and graduate degrees in technical fields from US universities are also valued.

IRAN

Iran is an oil-rich country of more than 80 million people east of the Persian Gulf. Over half of its population is Persian, not Arab. Nearly everyone is Muslim and nearly all Iranian Muslims are Shiite. The regime is a theocratic republic.

Unlike many of its neighboring countries, Iran has a national history stretching back to Classical times when the Persian civilization rivaled the Greeks.

POLITICAL CULTURE

The political culture is Muslim, based on Sharia law. However, there is an ancient foundation of Persian authoritarianism and an early 20th century overlay of democratic socialism.

Most people accept the authority of religious leaders and value a stable government that is involved in economic arenas. Individual rights are, to most people, secondary to the needs of the country.

Almost three-quarters of the people live in cities. Overall, Iranians are well educated (mostly in technical fields).

CLEAVAGES

The most obvious cleavage is between the dominant Shiites and the small groups of Sunni Muslims, who primarily live near the borders of the country. Politically, the division is of little importance. Similarly, ethnic cleavages have been bridged or suppressed during Iran's long history.

The urban-rural cleavage is more important because it coincides with much of the division between well-off and poor Iranians. The poor shanty towns on the fringes of cities reflect these divisions even though they are urban.

Politically, the most divisive cleavage is between the educated upper and middle classes, whose Islamic beliefs are less literal and whose practices are more casual than those of the less-educated lower class. This group of more secular Iranians is more likely to support democratic reforms and individual rights.

CIVIL SOCIETY

For most people civil society in Iran is centered on the local mosque and its imam. However, among the upper classes, professional organizations and private clubs are most important.

NGOs and human rights organizations function quietly and out of the public eye. Effective public leaders often end up in jail. The government acts quickly against any activity that might be political.

REGIME

The Iranian regime is a unitary system with some appearances of separation of powers. The Supreme Leader is chosen by the Assembly of Experts, a group of Muslim clerics elected by direct public vote. He is the head of state and commander of the armed forces and intelligence services. He appoints the head of the judiciary and many other government officials and is constitutionally the final word on government policies and actions.

The president is elected in a two-round majority vote, but candidates must be approved by a Guardian Council. Half of the Council is appointed by the Supreme Leader. The other half is appointed by the legislature. (The Council approves all candidates for elective offices.) The president is head of government and appoints local officials and directors of parastatals. His actions are subject to the approval of the Supreme Leader.

The administrative bureaucracy is made up of skilled and educated officials. However, they are observed by clerics who represent the Supreme Leader much like Chinese officials are observed by CPC cadres. Bureaucrats are suspect because their technical expertise is not based on Muslim law and learning.

The legislature, members of which are elected by two-round majority voting in single-member districts, can enact statute law and supervise the actions of the executive. The Majlis is a unicameral legislature whose actions can be vetoed by the Guardian Council or the Supreme Leader.

Courts deal with Sharia (Islamic) law and more modern civil and statutory law. All judges are clerics. It's an inquisitorial system that constitutionally is an independent power in the regime. It's the job of the judges and the investigative bureaucracies they supervise to identify crime, punish offenders, and reform criminals. There is a supreme court to which decisions can be appealed.

The Iranian military is an important arm of the government, but the Revolutionary Guards, a theocratic military force separate from the rest of the military, is one of the power centers in the regime. The Revolutionary Guards have close links to the clerical elite and the Supreme Leader.

Parastatals, mostly "charitable foundations" run by clerics or Revolutionary Guards, were created from corporations seized during the Islamic Revolution. Profits go to social welfare programs and to support loyal, conservative political forces.

PARTIES

Political parties are legal but not encouraged. Near elections, informal alliances are formed by groups supporting particular candidates, but their existence is only temporary. Behind the scenes, the political elite keep in touch with people they trust.

INTEREST GROUPS

Since political parties are discouraged, it should be expected that interest groups are as well. Lobbying is done personally at the highest levels of government. Groups that are part of the elite (e.g., top clergy and Revolutionary Guard commanders) are most likely to affect policy decisions.

MEDIA

All publications in Iran must have licenses from the government. These licenses can be revoked at any time.

The Islamic Republic of Iran Broadcasting is a parastatal that controls radio and television. Its head is appointed by the Supreme Leader. Some middle class and wealthy Iranians can afford access to satellite television.

Internet service providers in Iran must have a government license and every Web site must be registered. Since 2010, the government has been building a national network as a substitute for the Internet. Social media sites from outside of Iran are normally not accessible.

ECONOMY

Iran's GDP is just over $1 trillion (19th largest in the world) and its GDP per capita is $16,500 (96th highest in the world). Income distribution is slightly more unequal than Nigeria's or Russia's. About 19% of the people are considered to be living in poverty.

About a third of the economy is industrial and nearly half is in the service sector (largely government). Parastatals and charitable foundations dominate the economy. It is highly regulated and supervised.

In 2014, it's estimated that the government collected about 15% of GDP in taxes and had a budget deficit of about 1% of GDP. Military spending amounted to only 2.5% of GDP in 2012, because profits from many SOEs go to the military.

About half of government revenue came from oil sales, and about half of the Iranian economy is exempt from taxes because it's owned by charitable foundations (*bonyads*). Income and real estate taxes are the most common.

RECRUITMENT

Future leaders are found among the most loyal of followers in the clergy, the Revolutionary Guard, and the Basij. Some technocrats can demonstrate loyalty and earn popular support (e.g., Ahmadinejad) to rise to positions of power.

TAKING THE EXAM

REGISTERING FOR THE AP EXAM

If you are taking Comparative Government and Politics as an Advanced Placement course at your school, your teacher, counselor, or Advanced Placement coordinator will provide information about registering for the AP exam.

If your school does not offer the Comparative Government and Politics course, but does offer other AP courses, talk to your counselor or the school's AP coordinator about registering for the exam.

If you are home schooled or at a school that doesn't offer AP courses, you can still register and take the exam.

Go to

> https://apstudent.collegeboard.org/takingtheexam/
> registering-for-exams

When you contact AP services, you will get information about an AP coordinator near you who will accept your registration for the exam.

The deadline for registration is mid-March.

If you want to register for the AP exam outside of the USA, get more information and instructions at

> http://international.collegeboard.org/

DETAILS ABOUT THE EXAM

The AP web site offers good information about the exam and sample questions you can use for practice.

Go to

> https://apstudent.collegeboard.org/apcourse/
> ap-comparative-government-and-politics/
> about-the-exam

Basically, the exam consists of two equally weighted sections:

- The first section is made up of 55 multiple choice questions (to be completed in 45 minutes).

- The second section is made up of eight free response questions (to be completed in 100 minutes).

    * There are five short answer questions about basic concepts and facts from the countries you studied.

    * There is a conceptual question about a major concept requiring analysis of examples from the countries you studied.

    * There are two "Country Specific" questions, each one requiring analysis and specific examples from at least two of the countries you studied.

HINTS FOR TAKING THE EXAM

The multiple choice questions are carefully chosen and sorted. The test writers include some questions that they expect will be answered by 80% of the test takers. There are other questions that they expect will be answered by only 10-15% of test takers.

The exam instructions tell you to choose the **best** answer among the five alternatives on these questions.

There are no penalties for incorrect answers or unanswered questions.

The mean score for the multiple choice section of the exam is usually in the low 30s (out of 55 questions).

Sample multiple choice questions can be found online at

https://apstudent.collegeboard.org/apcourse/
ap-comparative-government-and-politics/exam-practice

The most common things you'll be asked to do on the Free Response Questions (FRQs) are

- describe
- explain
- identify
- define

You can find hints about what these verbs mean at

https://apstudent.collegeboard.org/apcourse/
ap-comparative-government-and-politics/exam-practice

At that URL, you'll also find FRQs used since 2006 AND the scoring guidelines for each of those questions.

ADDITIONAL RESOURCES

Need more than *Just the Facts?* For a comprehensive review of the material covered by AP Comparative Government and Politics course, go to

http://apcomparativegov.com

and order the 7th edition of *The AP Comparative Government and Politics Exam: What You Need to Know.* In addition to chapters on all six countries, there are chapters on the discipline of comparative politics, learning styles, and international organizations. Each one ends with a multiple-choice review quiz. At the end of the book, there is a full-length practice exam and an annotated key.

Online supplements include corrections, updates, and links to other sources, including

- *What You Need to Know* Facebook Group (for discussions and questions)
- *Teaching Comparative,* a Blog for Teachers

The **AP** *Comparative Government and Politics Examination

7th edition
revised & updated

What You Need to Know

A Test Preparation Guide by Ken Wedding, Regional Consultant to the College Board

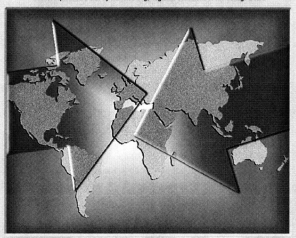

CPSIA information can be obtained
at www.ICGtesting.com
Printed in the USA
FFOW01n0047100418
46220560-47535FF

9 780996 578202